HARCOURT
Science

CALIFORNIA EDITION

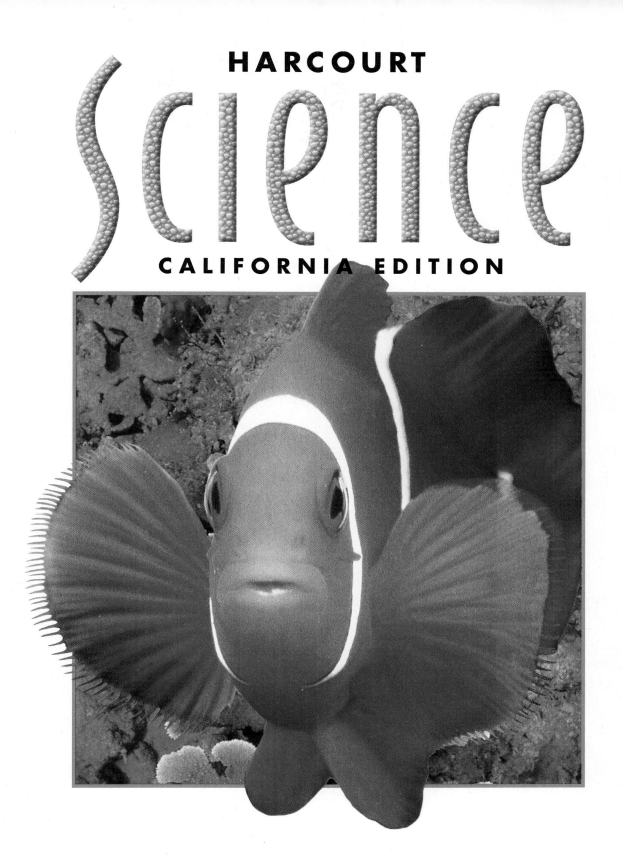

Harcourt School Publishers

Orlando • Boston • Dallas • Chicago • San Diego

www.harcourtschool.com

Cover Image

The clownfish lives in tropical
reefs of the Pacific Ocean.

ISBN 0-15-317649-0

7 8 9 10 11 12 032 10 09 08 07 06 05

Authors

Marjorie Slavick Frank
Former Adjunct Faculty Member at
    Hunter, Brooklyn, and Manhattan
    Colleges
New York, New York

Robert M. Jones
Professor of Education
University of Houston-Clear Lake
Houston, Texas

Gerald H. Krockover
Professor of Earth and Atmospheric
    Science Education
School Mathematics and Science
    Center
Purdue University
West Lafayette, Indiana

Mozell P. Lang
Science Education Consultant
Michigan Department of Education
Lansing, Michigan

Joyce C. McLeod
Visiting Professor
Rollins College
Winter Park, Florida

Carol J. Valenta
Vice President—Education,
    Exhibits, and Programs
St. Louis Science Center
St. Louis, Missouri
Former teacher, principal, and
    Coordinator of Science Center
    Instructional Programs
Los Angeles Unified School District
Los Angeles, California

Barry A. Van Deman
Science Program Director
Arlington, Virginia

Senior Editorial Advisor

Napoleon Adebola Bryant, Jr.
Professor Emeritus of Education
Xavier University
Cincinnati, Ohio

Program Advisors

Michael J. Bell
Assistant Professor of Early
    Childhood Education
School of Education
University of Houston-Clear Lake
Houston, Texas

George W. Bright
Professor of Mathematics Education
The University of North Carolina at
    Greensboro
Greensboro, North Carolina

Pansy Cowder
Science Specialist
Tampa, Florida

Robert H. Fronk
Head, Science/Mathematics
    Education Department
Florida Institute of Technology
Melbourne, Florida

Gloria R. Guerrero
Education Consultant
Specialist in English as a Second
    Language
San Antonio, Texas

Bernard A. Harris, Jr.
Physician and Former Astronaut
(STS 55—*Space Shuttle Columbia*,
STS 63—*Space Shuttle Discovery*)
Vice President, SPACEHAB Inc.
Houston, Texas

Lois Harrison-Jones
Education and Management
    Consultant
Dallas, Texas

Linda Levine
Educational Consultant
Orlando, Florida

Kenneth R. Mechling
Professor of Biology and Science
    Education
Clarion University of Pennsylvania
Clarion, Pennsylvania

Barbara ten Brink
Science Director
Round Rock Independent School
    District
Round Rock, Texas

Reviewers and Contributors

Kimberly Gay
Teacher, Mango Elementary School
Seffner, Florida

Marilyn Hamen
Teacher, Bear Creek Elementary
Grapevine-Colleyville ISD
Euless, Texas

Natalia Lasher
Teacher, Simonds Elementary
San Jose, California

Michael F. Ryan
Educational Technology Specialist
Lake County Schools
Tavares, Florida

Shari Lynn Snyder
Teacher, Piney Grove Elementary
    School
Charlotte, North Carolina

Judy Taylor
Teacher, Silvestri Junior High School
Las Vegas, Nevada

UNIT A

Life Science

About Living Things

UNIT A

Life Science
(continued)

★5

Earth Science

Weather and the Seasons

Extension Chapters

Introduction and References

Using Science Skills

Observe

Compare

Sequence

Classify

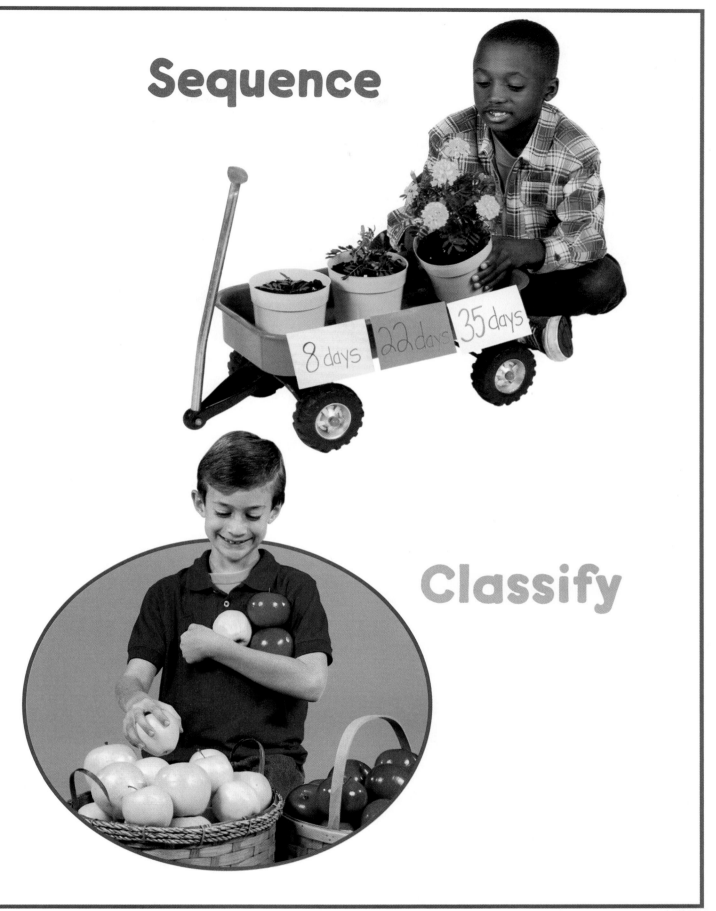

8 days   22 days   35 days

Infer

Gather Information

Plan

Make Models

Measure

Predict

Draw Conclusions

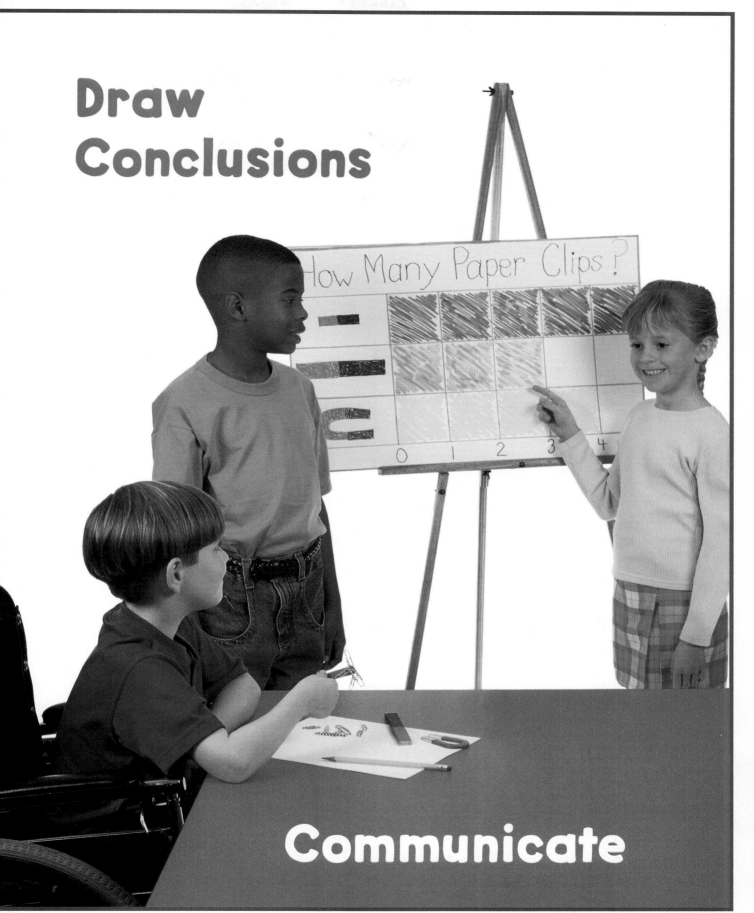

How Many Paper Clips?

0 1 2 3 4

Communicate

Science Safety

Think ahead.

Be neat.

Be careful.

Do not eat or drink things.

Safety Symbols

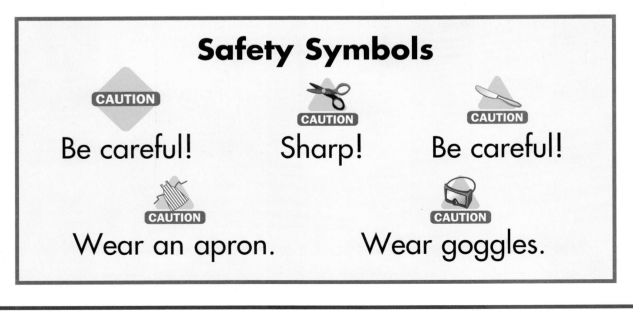

CAUTION Be careful!

CAUTION Sharp!

CAUTION Be careful!

CAUTION Wear an apron.

CAUTION Wear goggles.

About Living Things

Life Science

About Living Things

UNIT PROJECT

Watch Me Grow!

Plan a class aquarium. Find out what things plants and animals need to live there.

CHAPTER 1

Living and Nonliving Things

Vocabulary

senses
living
nonliving

Did You Know?
Dogs have **senses** as people do, but dogs can hear higher sounds.

The oldest **living** thing on Earth is the bristlecone pine tree in the United States.

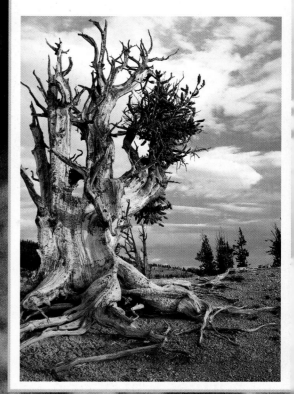

How Do My Senses Help Me Learn?

Investigate

Using Your Senses

You will need

pieces of fruit   plastic gloves

1 Close your eyes. Your partner will put on gloves and give you a piece of fruit.

2 Touch and smell the fruit. Tell what you observe. Name the fruit.

3 Take turns with your partner.

Science Skill

When you observe things, use more than your eyes to find out about them.

Your Five Senses

You have five **senses** that help you learn about things. What part of your body do you use for each sense?

sight

smell

touch

hearing

taste

Sight

Your sense of sight helps you learn how things look.

■ **What can the boy learn by looking at the fish?**

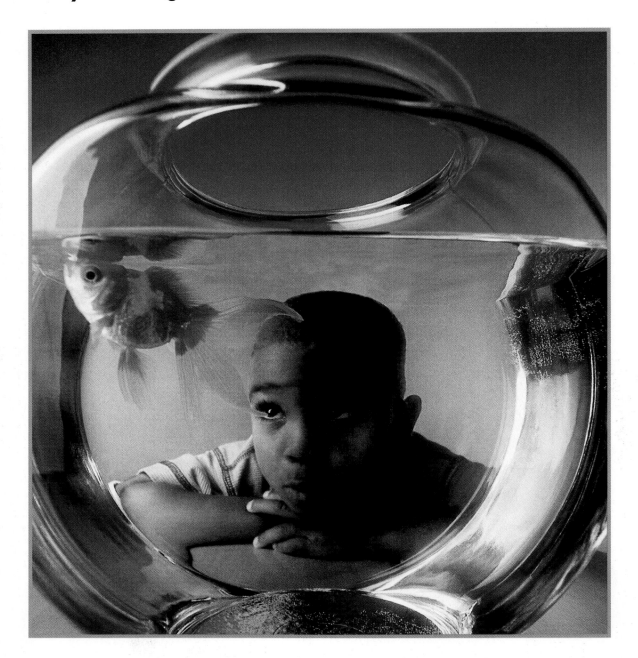

Touch

Your sense of touch helps you learn how things feel.

■ **What can the girl learn by touching the kitten?**

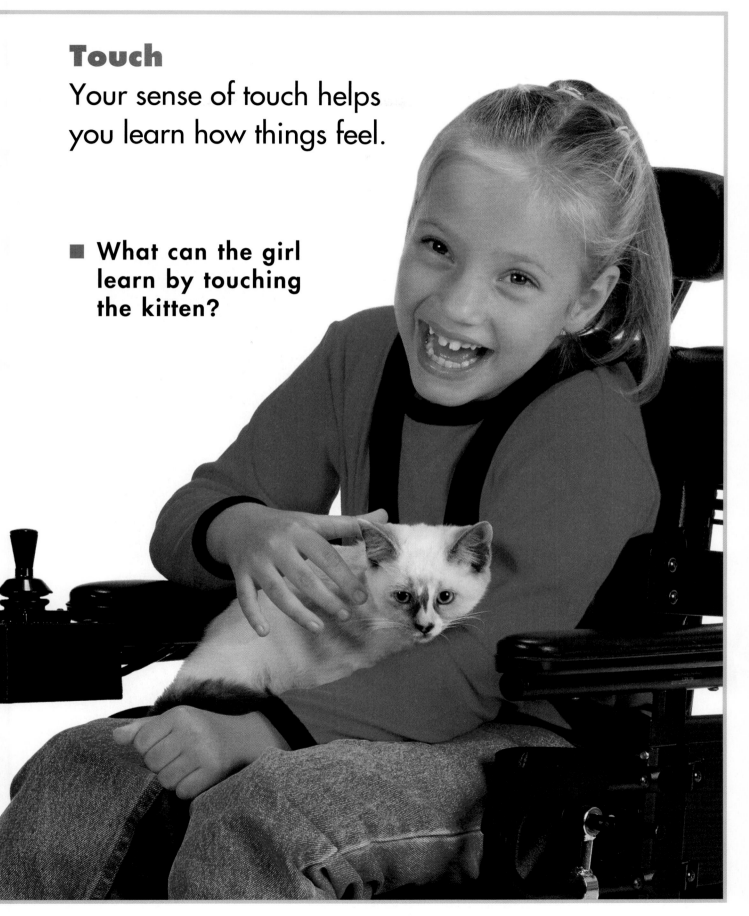

Hearing

Your sense of hearing helps
you learn about sounds.

■ **What sound does
this boy hear?**

Smell

Your sense of smell helps you learn how things smell.

■ **How do you think these flowers smell?**

Taste

Your sense of taste helps you choose what to eat.

■ **How do you think these grapes taste?**

Think About It

1. What are the five senses?
2. How do your senses help you learn?

What Are Living and Nonliving Things?

A Mealworm and a Rock

You will need

mealworm

rock

hand lens

bran meal

1 Give bran meal to the mealworm and the rock. Use the hand lens to observe.

2 Does the mealworm or the rock move or eat? Draw what you see.

3 Compare the mealworm and the rock. Which is a living thing?

Science Skill

When you compare things, you tell how they are the same and different.

Living and Nonliving Things

Plants, animals, and people are **living** things. They need food, water, and air to live and grow. **Nonliving** things do not need food, water, and air.

nonliving

living

Living Things

Flowers and dogs are living things. They need food, water, and air to grow and change. They come from other living things.

■ **How do you know the flower is a living thing?**

Nonliving Things

A rock and a chair are nonliving things.
They do not need food, water, and air.
They do not grow.

■ **How can you tell these are nonliving things?**

Compare Living and Nonliving Things

How can you tell if something is living?
Ask these questions.

- Does it need food, water, and air?
- Does it grow and change?

If you say yes both times, the thing is living.

- How are these bears the same?
- How are they different?

These pictures show living things and nonliving things. Water can move, but it is a nonliving thing. It does not need food and air.

■ **Which things in these pictures are living and nonliving?**

Think About It

1. What is a living thing?

2. What is a nonliving thing?

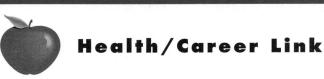

A Doctor Observes People

This doctor is using her senses as she gives the boy a checkup. She listens to his heart. She looks at his throat.

■ **Which sense is the doctor using in each picture?**

Think and Do

Draw a picture of a doctor. Then show your picture. Tell how doctors use their senses in their work.

Math Link

Measure with a Growth Chart

This girl can tell she is growing. Her mother measures her on a growth chart. She is taller now than she was a year ago.

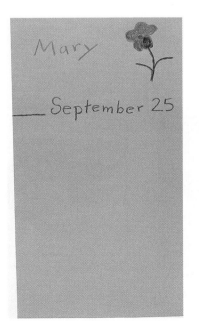

Mary

_____ September 25

Think and Do

Make a growth chart. Have someone help you mark how tall you are. Write the date. Measure how tall you are each month.

Tell What You Know

1. Which senses would you use to learn more about each thing?

Vocabulary

Tell which pictures go with the words.

2. living thing

3. nonliving thing

a.   b.   c.   d.

Using Science Skills

4. Observe Collect things in an egg carton. Use two words to tell how each thing feels, looks, sounds, or smells. Have a partner guess each thing.

5. Compare Make a chart to compare a pencil and a plant. Draw pictures of them. Tell if the things are living or nonliving.

Living or Nonliving?			
Thing	Picture	Does it need air and water?	Does it grow?
pencil			
plant			

CHAPTER 2

All About Plants

Vocabulary

root
stem
leaves
flower
seed
seed coat
sunlight

Did You Know?
The rafflesia is the biggest **flower** in the world.

Did You Know?
There is a plant that has **leaves** that look like elephant ears.

What Are the Parts of a Plant?

Plant Parts

You will need

carrot

plant with flower

paper and pencil

1 Look at the parts of one plant. Draw what you see.

2 Look at the parts of the other plant. Draw what you see.

3 Compare the plants. Tell about their parts.

Science Skill
When you compare things, you tell how they are the same and different.

Parts of a Plant

Plants have different parts. Most plants have roots, a stem, and leaves. Many plants also have flowers.

flower

leaf

stem

roots

How Plant Parts Help a Plant

Plants have many shapes and sizes.
Most plants have the same parts.
These parts help them live and grow.

Roots

The **roots** hold
plants in the soil. The
roots also take in water.

■ **What part of a carrot
do you eat?**

■ **Where are the stems in these pictures?**

Stems

The **stem** helps hold up the plant. Water moves up the stem to the leaves.

A tree trunk is also a stem. Water moves up the trunk to the tree's leaves.

Leaves

The **leaves** make food for the plant. Leaves from different plants have different shapes.

■ **What shapes do you see?**

Flowers

Many plants also have flowers.
The **flowers** make seeds.

■ **What part of the plant is this bee on?**

Think About It

1. How are plants the same?

2. How are they different?

How Do Plants Grow?

The Inside of a Seed

You will need

bean seed

hand lens

1 Peel off the covering of the seed.

2 Open the seed.

3 Observe. Tell what is inside.

Science Skill

Use a hand lens to help you observe.

How Plants Grow

Most plants grow from a **seed**. The seed may have a covering called a **seed coat**. The seed coat falls away as the plant grows.

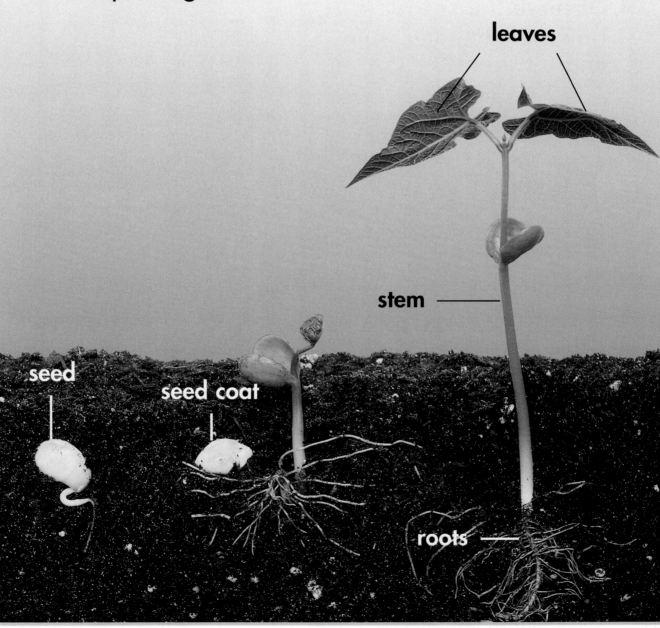

leaves

stem

seed

seed coat

roots

Plants Grow from Seeds

Different plants grow from different seeds. The new plants look like the plants the seeds came from. When old plants die, their seeds can be planted to grow new plants.

■ **Observe the seeds. How are they the same and different?**

tomato seeds

sunflower seeds

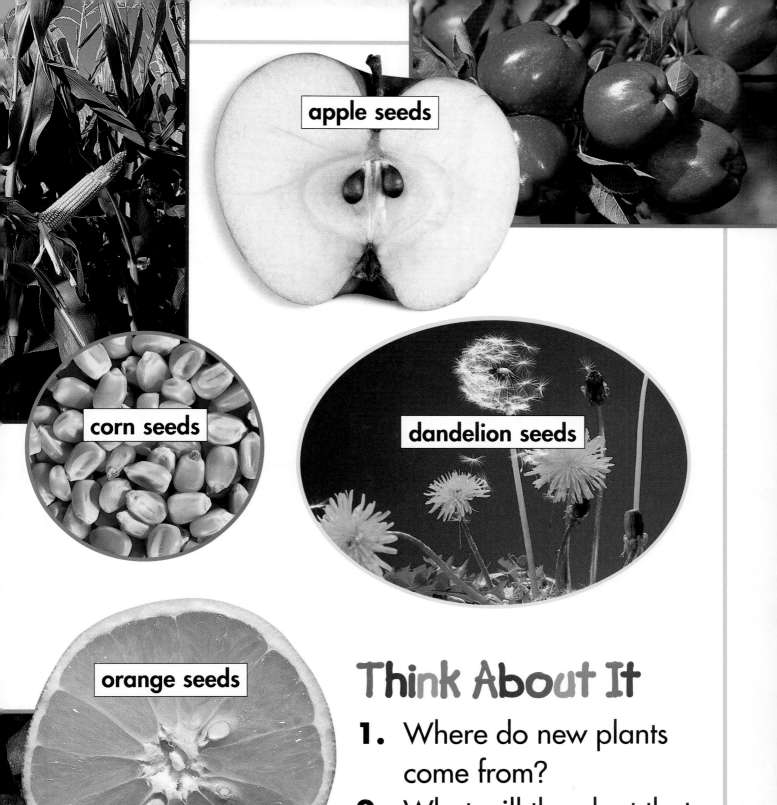

apple seeds

corn seeds

dandelion seeds

orange seeds

Think About It

1. Where do new plants come from?
2. What will the plant that grows from a seed look like?

What Do Plants Need?

What Plants Need to Grow

You will need

seeds

2 clear cups

any color cup

soil

1 Fill one clear cup with soil. Plant two seeds near the side. Water.

2 Put the cup with the seeds into the cup with color. After 3 days, take it out.

3 Share what you see.

Science Skill
When you share your ideas, you **communicate** with others.

What Plants Need to Live

Plants need three things to live and grow.
What are these three things?

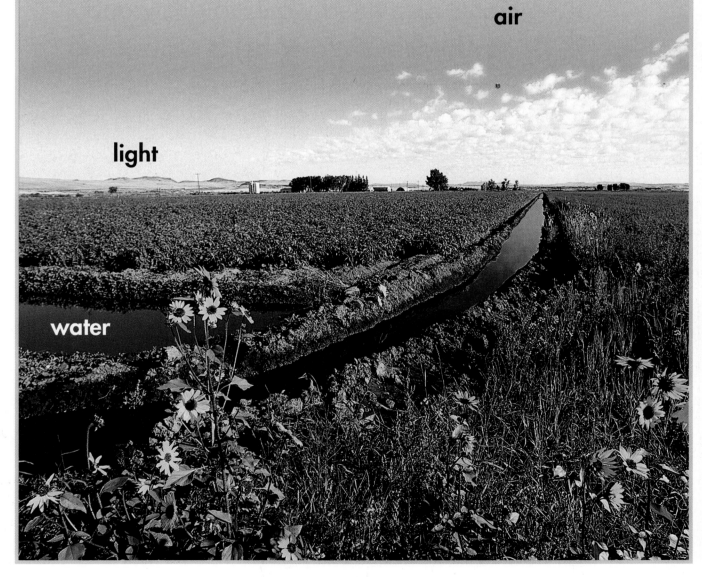

air

light

water

How Plants Grow and Live

Light and Air

A plant's leaves use light and air to make the plant's food. Light from the sun is called **sunlight**.

Water

Plants also need water to grow and stay healthy. Water helps move food to all parts of the plant.

■ How do this plant's leaves help the plant live?

Different kinds of plants grow in different places around the world. All these plants need light, air, and water.

■ **Where is the water in each of these pictures?**

Think About It

1. What do plants need to live and grow?

2. How do leaves use light and air?

Art Link

An Artist Observes Plants

An artist named Vincent van Gogh painted these flowers long ago. Artists look closely at things around them.

Sunflowers by Vincent van Gogh

■ **What parts of a plant can you see in this picture?**

■ **What part is missing?**

Flower

Stem

Think and Do

Paint your own picture of a plant. Show at least two parts.

Measure a Plant

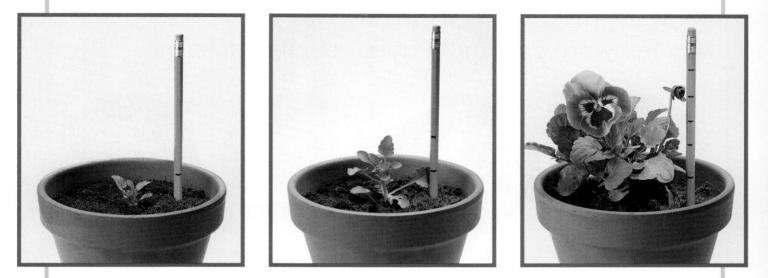

You can use a ruler to measure how tall a plant grows. You can also use a pencil or a stick if you do not have a ruler.

Think and Do

Watch a plant grow. Put a pencil down in the soil next to the plant. Mark how tall the plant is. Every three days, mark how much the plant has grown.

Tell What You Know

1. Tell what you know about each picture.

Vocabulary

Tell which picture goes with each word or words.

2. roots

3. leaves

4. stem

5. flowers

6. sunlight

7. seed

8. seed coat

a. b. c. d.

e. f. g.

Using Science Skills

9. **Compare** Roots take in water. Stems help plants stand up. Think about the parts of your body that take in water or help you stand up. How are you the same as a plant? How are you different?

10. **Observe** Make a chart about leaves where you live.

   Find two leaves. Glue or tape them on your chart. Tell about your leaves.

Leaves			
Leaf	Shape	Color	Size

CHAPTER 3

All About Animals

Vocabulary

gills

mammal

reptile

amphibian

insect

hatch

larva

pupa

tadpole

Did You Know?
A gecko is a
reptile that can
crawl up trees.

Did You Know?
There are more kinds of beetles than any other kind of **insect**.

What Do Animals Need?

An Animal Home

You will need

plastic box
and gloves

soil, twig,
and rocks

water in a
bottle cap

small
animals

1 Put the soil, twig,
rocks, water, and
animals in the box.

2 Observe. How does your
home give the animals
food, water, and a place
to hide?

3 Draw what you see.
Close the lid.

Science Skill

When you observe the
animals in their home,
you can see how they
meet their needs.

What Animals Need

All animals need food, water, air, and a place to live. These ducks live by a pond. Why is this a good home for them?

mallard ducks

horse

Animals Need Food

Different kinds of animals need different kinds of food to live and grow. Horses eat grass, but lions eat meat. A horse's flat teeth are good for chewing grass. A lion's sharp teeth are good for tearing meat.

■ **What do an animal's teeth tell you about what it eats?**

mountain lion

Animals Need Water

All animals need water to live. Like many animals, a camel drinks with its mouth. It also gets water from the food it eats. An elephant uses its trunk to put water in its mouth.

■ **How are the camels and the elephant getting the water they need?**

camels

elephant

Animals Need a Place To Live

All animals need a place to live. Some find homes. Others build homes. Animals keep safe and raise their young in their homes.

bat

peregrine falcons

Park Ranger

Many animals have homes in parks. If they need help, park rangers take care of them.

Animals Need Air

All animals need air to live and grow. Special body parts help them get it. Some animals have a nose and lungs. Others, like this fish, have **gills** that take air from water.

cow

gills

Think About It

1. What do animals need to live and grow?

2. What are some ways animals meet these needs?

What Are Some Kinds of Animals?

Animals in Your Neighborhood

You will need

paper and pencil

1 Observe different kinds of animals in your schoolyard.

2 Draw a picture of each animal you observe.

3 Classify the animals into groups. How are the animals in each group the same?

Science Skill

When you classify animals, you observe how they are the same. Then you group them.

reptile

Different Kinds of Animals

Scientists observe how animals are the same and different. They put animals that are the same into groups. Here are some kinds of animals.

birds

fish

mammal

amphibian

Mammals

A **mammal** is an animal that feeds its young milk. A mammal also has hair or fur on its body.

■ How can you tell these animals are mammals?

whitetail deer

pig

squirrel

Birds

Birds are animals that have two wings and two feet. They are the only animals that have feathers. Some birds fly, some birds run, and some swim.

macaw

bluebird

flamingo

■ **How are all these birds the same?**

Reptiles

A **reptile** is an animal with rough, dry skin. It may have scales or hard plates. Alligators and turtles are reptiles.

alligators

giant tortoise

Amphibians

An **amphibian** is an animal with smooth, wet skin. Frogs, toads, and salamanders are amphibians.

salamander

■ How are amphibians different from reptiles?

Fish

Fish live in water. They have special body parts called gills that help them breathe. Their bodies are covered with scales.

snapper

gills

queen angelfish

■ **How are these fish the same?**

Think About It

1. What are some different kinds of animals?

2. How are the animals in all the groups the same? How are they different?

What Are Insects?

A Model of an Insect

You will need

Styrofoam balls   scissors

toothpicks
and chenille sticks   wax paper

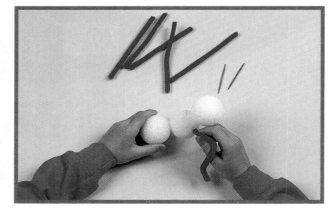

1 Choose an insect to make. Insects have three body parts and six legs.

2 Choose materials. Make a model of your insect.

CAUTION Be careful with toothpicks, chenille sticks, and scissors. They are sharp.

3 Compare your model with a picture of a real insect.

Science Skill

When you make a model of an insect, you show parts that a real insect has.

A54

Insects

An **insect** is an animal that has three body parts and six legs. Some insects also have wings.

3 body parts

weevil

More About Insects

Insects lay eggs. A ladybug lays hundreds of eggs at one time.

Insects do not have bones. They have a strong body covering. The covering keeps their soft insides safe.

ladybug

■ **What else do you think the body covering does for the grasshopper?**

grasshopper

A butterfly is an insect. It uses its wings to fly. An ant is an insect, too. Most ants have no wings. They use their legs to move fast.

■ **How are the butterfly and the ant the same and different?**

butterfly

ant

Think About It

1. How can you tell if an animal is an insect?

2. What else do you know about insects?

How Do Animals Grow?

Investigate

Animals and Their Young

You will need

animal
picture cards

paper and
pencil

Animals and Their Young		
Animal	Same	Different
cats	Both have ears. Both are orange.	One is big. One is small.

1 Match the picture cards. Put each young animal with the adult.

2 Make a chart. Compare the young animal and the adult.

3 Tell how each young animal is like the adult. Tell how it is different.

Science Skill

When you compare the pictures, you tell how they are the same and different.

How Different Kinds of Animals Grow

These young animals will change as they get older. They will grow to look like their parents.

bunny

chick

Ways Animals Begin Life

Rabbits are small when they are born. Their eyes are closed. They can not walk or hop until they are older.

just born

8 days old

■ **How do the chick and the rabbit change in different ways?**

Chicks **hatch**, or break out of eggs. Their eyes are open. Soon they can walk and peck for food.

just hatched

8 days old

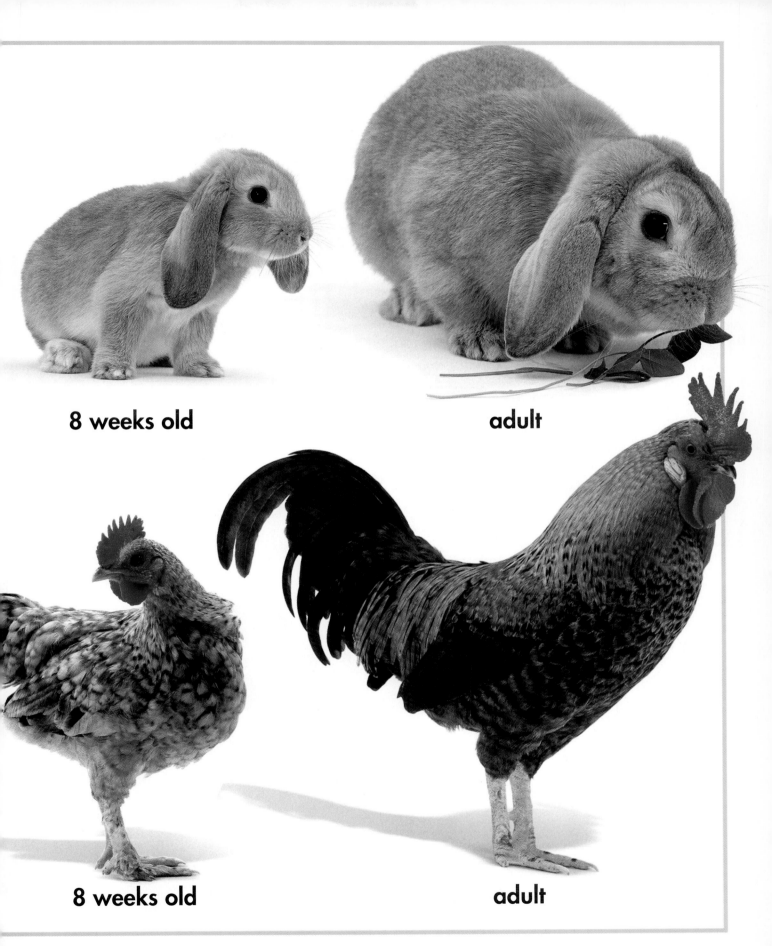

8 weeks old

adult

8 weeks old

adult

Animals Care for Their Young

Some animals feed their young. Later they teach them how to find food.

robins

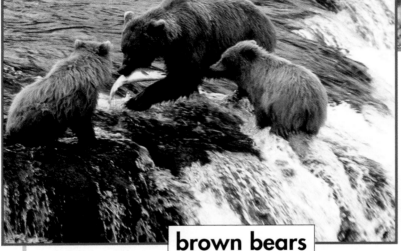

brown bears

■ **How do these animals make sure their young have food?**

Some animals lick their young to clean them. Later they show them how to clean themselves.

chimpanzees

Some animals stay close to their young to keep them warm. Others keep their young warm in pouches.

■ **How do these penguins keep their baby warm?**

emperor penguins

Think About It

1. What are two ways that animals begin life?
2. How do all young animals change as they grow?

How Does a Butterfly Grow?

A Butterfly's Life

You will need

box   caterpillar   paper and pencil

1 Keep your caterpillar in a warm place.

2 Observe your caterpillar every day for three weeks. Draw it each time.

3 How did your caterpillar change? Share what happened.

Science Skill

When you use your senses to observe, you find out how the caterpillar changes.

How a Butterfly Grows

A butterfly is an insect. It hatches from an egg. It changes many times before it grows colorful wings. What do all insects have?

monarch butterfly

From Caterpillar to Butterfly

A butterfly begins life as an egg. A tiny caterpillar, or **larva**, hatches from the egg. The caterpillar eats and grows.

1 egg

2 caterpillar or larva

3 pupa

4
butterfly
comes out

Then it stops eating. The caterpillar becomes a **pupa** and makes a hard covering.

Inside the covering, the pupa slowly changes. Finally a butterfly comes out and flies away.

5 adult butterfly

Wings Help Butterflies Keep Safe

Butterfly wings have different shapes and colors. Some wings look like leaves or flowers. These wings help butterflies hide.

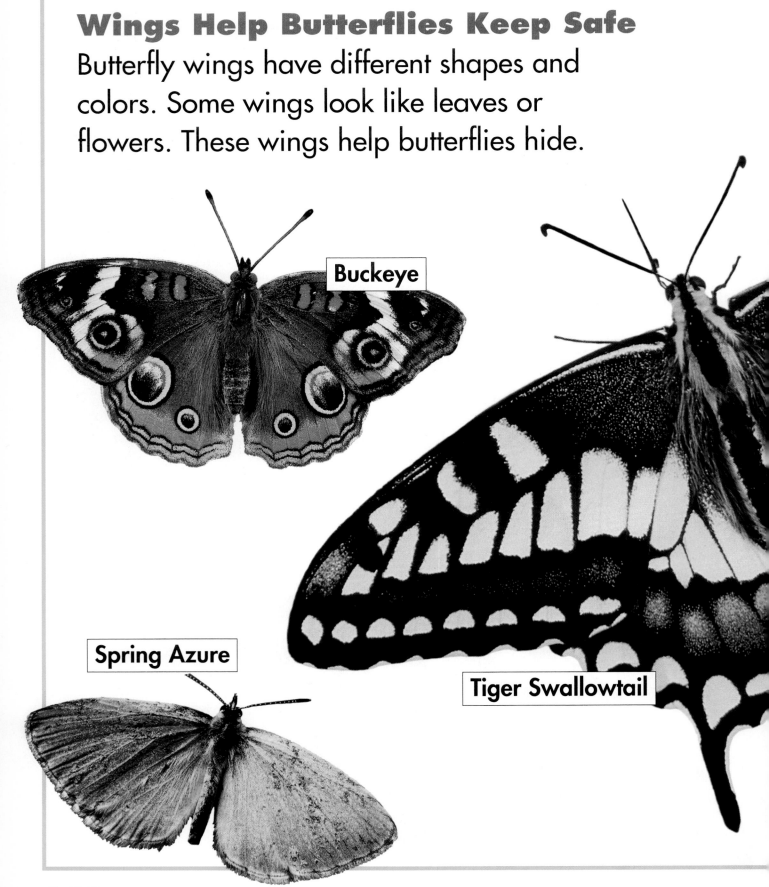

Buckeye

Spring Azure

Tiger Swallowtail

Other wings help butterflies trick hungry birds.

■ **How do you think "eye spots" might trick a bird?**

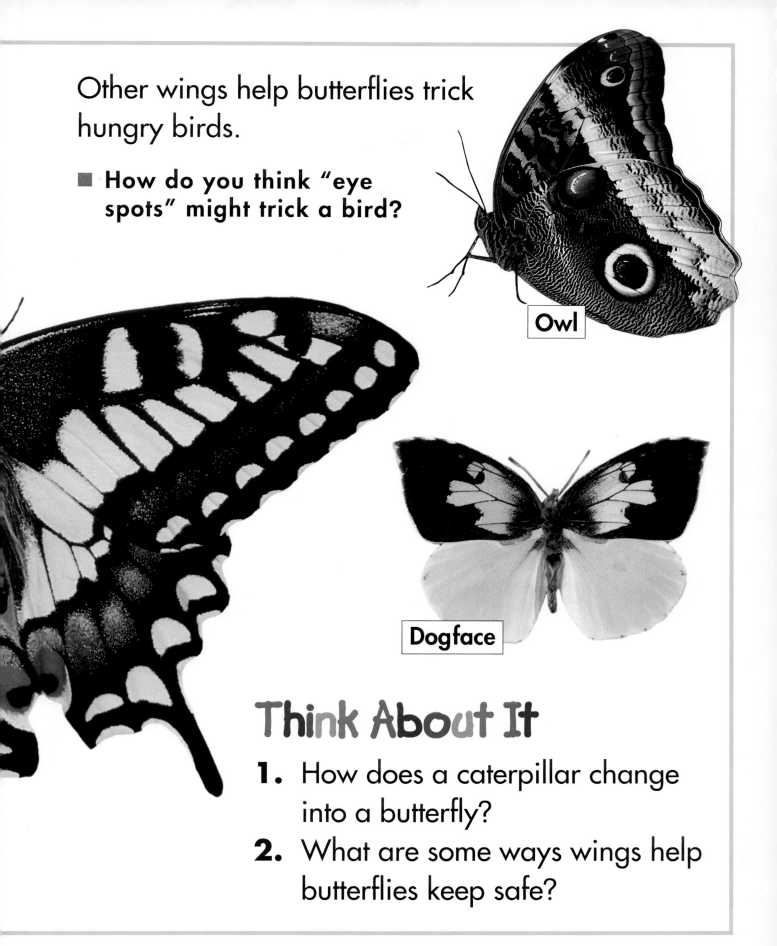

Owl

Dogface

Think About It

1. How does a caterpillar change into a butterfly?
2. What are some ways wings help butterflies keep safe?

How Does a Frog Grow?

A Frog's Life

You will need

picture cards

1 Put the picture cards in sequence. Show how you think a frog changes as it grows.

2 Tell why you put your cards in the order you did.

Science Skill

When you sequence the cards, you show what happens first, next, and last.

How a Frog Grows

A frog is an amphibian. It hatches from an egg. As it grows, it changes many times. When it is an adult, it has long back legs.

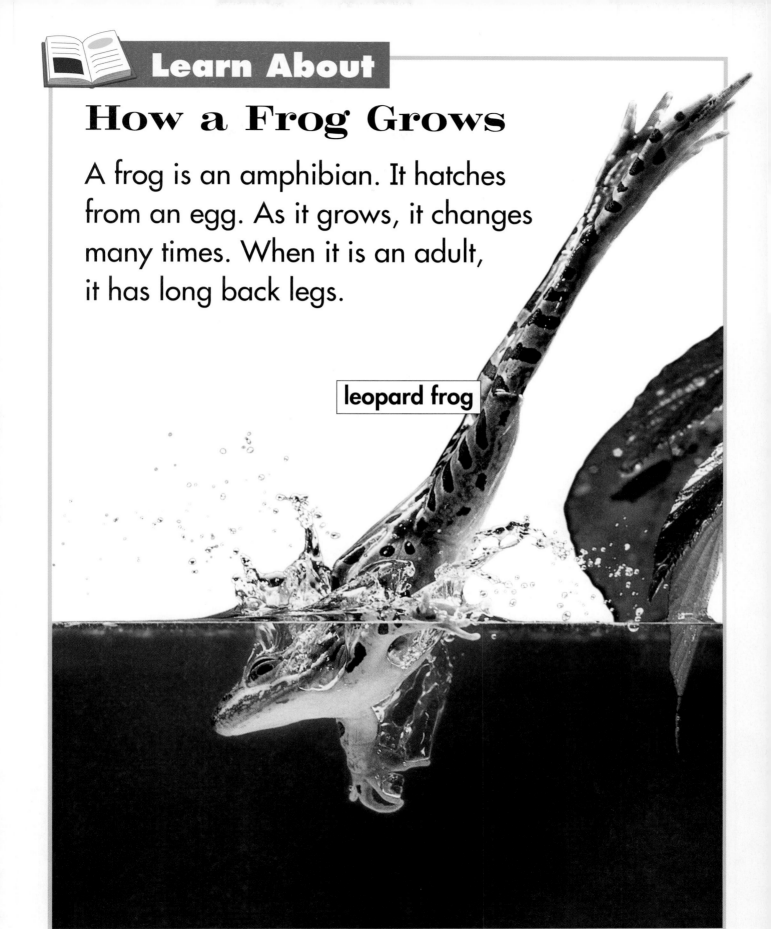

leopard frog

From Tadpole to Frog

Frogs lay their eggs in water. Young frogs, or **tadpoles**, hatch from the eggs. They have tails to move and gills to breathe in water. They grow.

■ How has this tadpole changed?

3 tadpole with back legs

2 tadpole

1 frog eggs

The tadpoles keep changing. They grow front legs. They get lungs to breathe air. Their tails get smaller. Then they look like little frogs. They climb onto land and grow bigger.

tadpole grows front legs, tail gets smaller

5 adult frog

Think About It

1. How does a tadpole change into a frog?
2. What body parts does a tadpole have that a frog does not have?

Movement/Drama Link

Move Like a Frog

These children think about a time in a frog's life. Then they move to show what that time is like.

Think and Do

Find an open space on the floor. Show what a frog does as an egg, a tadpole, or an adult frog.

Math Link

Find Symmetry

Look at this butterfly's wings. Find the two parts that match. Use your finger to trace a line between the matching parts.

Think and Do

Make a butterfly with wings that match.

Fold a paper plate in half. Open the plate, and paint patterns on one half. While the paint is wet, press the two halves together. Then open the plate.

How are the two parts the same?

Tell What You Know

1. Tell how these animals are the same. Then tell how they are different.

Vocabulary

Tell which picture goes with each word.

2. mammal

3. reptile

4. amphibian

5. insect

6. gills

7. pupa

8. tadpole

9. hatch

10. larva

a.   **b.**   **c.**

d.   **e.**   **f.**

g.   **h.**   **i.**

Using Science Skills

11. Classify Make a bar graph to show groups of animals. Find pictures of animals. Classify your pictures to make a graph like this one.

Animal Groups

Number

Kinds of Animals

| Insects | Amphibians | Mammals | Fish | Reptiles | Birds |

12. Sequence A butterfly changes as it grows. Write the words in sequence to show how this insect changes.

adult butterfly

larva

egg

pupa

Senses Game

Get a box and put in different things. Ask your family or classmates to close their eyes. Have them use touch and hearing to guess each thing.

Nature Walk

Take a nature walk with your class or with family members. Draw or write about what you observe.

Compare Two Plants

Cut off one plant just above the soil and at the bottom of the stems. Plant the cut stems in a new pot of soil. Put it on a table next to the other potted plant. Label and water both plants. Observe what happens.

Observe a Pet

With an adult, find a pet to observe. Draw or write about the animal.

What does the pet look like?

What does it eat and drink?

Plants and Animals Need One Another

Vocabulary

shelter

enrich

pollen

product

Did You Know?
Some animals such as the clownfish use other animals for shelter.

Did You Know?
Ragweed **pollen** has sharp points that make people sneeze.

How Do Animals Need Plants?

Investigate

How Small Animals Use Plants

You will need

timer or watch   string loop   paper and pencil

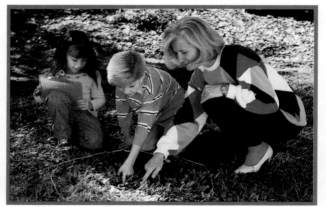

1 Go outside with your class. Observe animals and plants inside your string loop.

2 Observe and record for five minutes. How are animals using plants?

3 Share what you observed.

Science Skill

As you observe, use your senses of sight, hearing, and smell to help you.

Some animals eat other animals as well as plants. A toucan eats insects as well as fruit. A raccoon eats both fish and berries.

■ **What is this raccoon eating?**

raccoon

toucan

Other Ways Animals Need Plants

Some animals need plants for shelter. A **shelter** is a place where an animal can be safe.

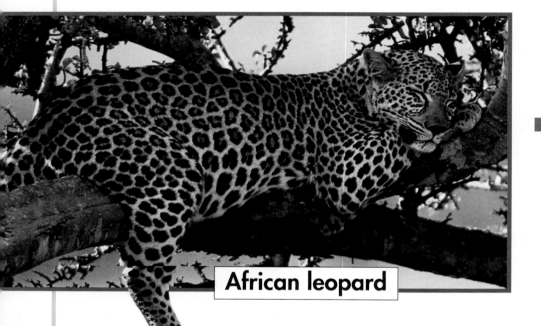

African leopard

■ **How does the tree help this leopard keep safe?**

termites

Many animals that live in the soil need plants for shelter. They may live inside rotting logs. They eat bits of dead plants.

Some animals make nests with parts of plants. A bird may use grass. An alligator uses leaves and strong reeds.

oriole

alligator

deer mice

■ **What do mice use to make a nest?**

Think About It

1. What are some ways animals need plants?

2. What animals eat only plants? What animals eat other animals as well as plants?

How Do Animals Help Plants?

How Seeds Stick to Animals

You will need

Styrofoam ball

glue

cotton and other materials to try out

1 Look at this picture. How might these seeds stick to animals?

2 Plan a model of a seed that sticks. Choose materials to glue to the ball.

3 Investigate your materials. Which ones stick to the cotton? The cotton is like animal fur.

Science Skill

To investigate how seeds stick to animals, make a plan to try out different ideas. Follow your plan.

How Animals Help Plants

Some animals carry seeds to new places. Some help make the soil better for plants. Others help flowers make seeds.

Animals Carry Seeds

A seed may stick to a cat's fur. The seed may be carried far from the plant. When the seed falls off, it may grow into a new plant.

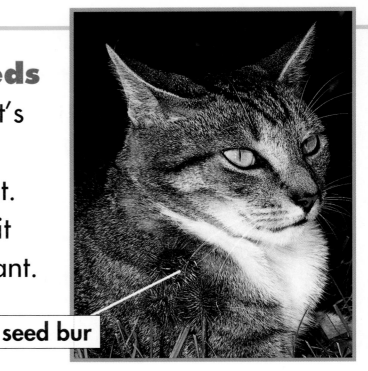

seed bur

Animals Help Make Soil Better

earthworm

A worm eats dead plants. Its waste helps **enrich** the soil, or make the soil better for plants.

■ **What things are these animals doing that help plants?**

Animals Help Plants Make Seeds

Flowers have a powder called **pollen** that helps them make seeds. A butterfly carries pollen from flower to flower. The pollen falls off. Those flowers use the pollen to make seeds.

butterfly

Think About It

1. How do small animals make the soil better for plants?
2. How do animals help plants grow new plants?

How Do We Need Plants and Animals?

Investigate

Things People Use

You will need

picture cards

1 Which pictures show things made from plants? Which are from animals?

2 Classify the cards. Sort them into groups.

3 Share your groups. Tell why each thing belongs.

Science Skill

When you classify the things on the cards, you group them to show ways they are the same.

How People Need Plants and Animals

People need plants and animals for food, clothing, and shelter. Plants and animals also add beauty to people's lives.

What People Need Plants For

People need shelter and clothing. They use plants to make many products. A **product** is something that people make from other things.

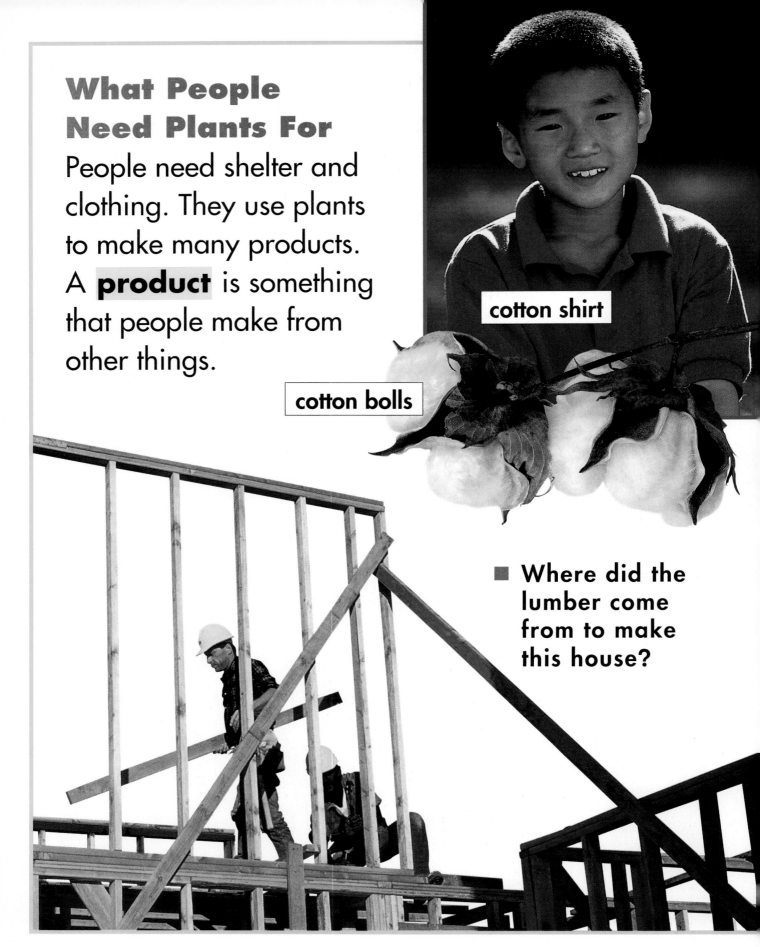

cotton shirt

cotton bolls

■ Where did the lumber come from to make this house?

People eat parts of plants. Celery is the stem of a plant. Peanut butter is made from peanuts, the seeds of a plant.

■ **What plant do you like to eat?**

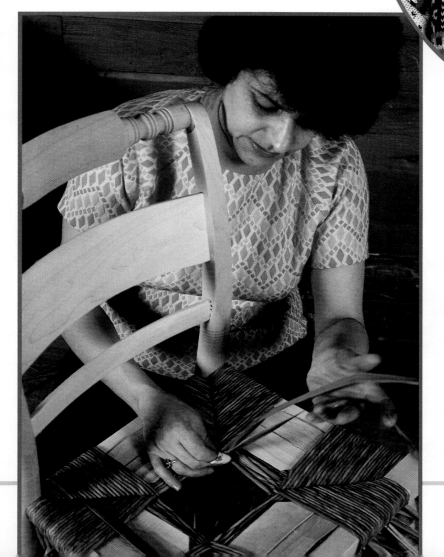

People also use plants to make products they need in their homes.

What People Need Animals For

People use animals for food. Many people eat beef, pork, chicken, and fish. Eggs and milk are also foods from animals.

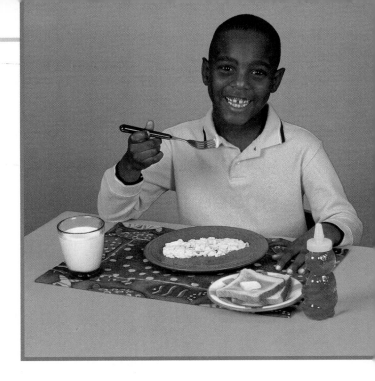

■ **What parts of this breakfast come from animals? What parts come from plants?**

People use wool from sheep to make clothing. Coats and sweaters may be made with wool.

Some people keep animals as pets. Others need animals as helpers. Guide dog trainers work with some dogs. They teach them to help people who are blind.

Think About It

1. What are some ways people need plants?

2. What are some ways people need animals?

Math Link

Snacks Made from Plants

People make snacks from plants. They mix nuts, dried fruits, and cereal to make a tasty treat. Stores may call this snack *trail mix.*

Think and Do

Make a snack from plants. Measure one cup each of granola, raisins, and nuts into a bowl. Mix them. Eat your trail mix snack.

Keeping a Custom

Long ago, some African Americans in South Carolina made baskets like this one. They wove them from plants. This woman keeps the custom. She weaves a basket as people did long ago.

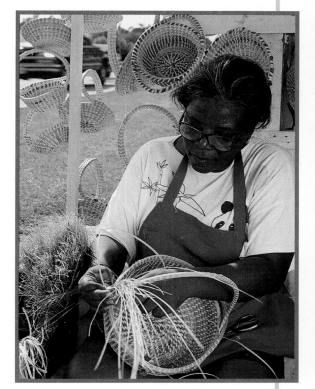

Think and Do

Paper comes from plants. It is made from the wood of trees. Use strips of colored paper to weave a place mat.

Tell What You Know

1. Tell how animals and people can use these plants to meet their needs.

Vocabulary

Tell which picture goes with each word. Then use the word to tell about the picture.

a.   **b.**

2. enrich

3. shelter

4. pollen

5. product

c.   **d.**

Using Science Skills

6. **Classify** Collect pictures of different kinds of foods. Put the foods that come from plants in one group. Put the foods that come from animals in another group.

   What foods can you find that come from both plants and animals?

7. **Observe** Make a chart about the ways you use plants and animals. Observe ways you use them at school. Draw pictures in your chart.

Ways I Use Plants and Animals			
	Food	Clothing	Beauty
Plants			
Animals			

5

A Place to Live

Vocabulary

forest
desert
rain forest
ocean
algae

Did You Know?
Squirrels in the **desert** use their tails like beach umbrellas to stay cool.

Did You Know?
A plant called **algae** is used to make ice cream.

What Lives in a Forest?

Forest Trees

You will need

dark crayon   pencil and paper

1 Go outside. Find a tree. Draw one of its leaves.

2 Make a rubbing of the tree's bark.

3 Compare your drawing and rubbing with a classmate's.

Science Skill

When you compare drawings and rubbings, look for ways the trees are the same and different.

Forests

A **forest** is a place where many trees grow. A forest floor is shady. The soil stays moist.

forest

Forest Plants and Animals

Some trees grow tall in a forest. Their high leaves catch the sunlight they need to make food.

Berry bushes and mountain laurels need less sunlight than trees. They can grow below the trees.

berry bushes

mountain laurel

Many animals find food and shelter in a forest. Wood thrushes find safe places to build their nests. Box turtles eat worms for food.

wood thrushes

red foxes

■ How are the foxes meeting their needs?

box turtle

Think About It

1. What is a forest?
2. How do plants and animals in a forest meet their needs?

What Lives in the Desert?

Desert Leaves

You will need

2 paper clips

water

wax paper

2 paper-towel leaf shapes

1 Make both leaf shapes damp. Put one shape on wax paper. Fold the paper over. Clip it.

2 Put both leaves in the sunlight. Check them after an hour.

3 Which leaf holds water longer? Draw a conclusion.

Science Skill

To draw a conclusion about desert leaves, think about your leaf with the waxy coat and the other leaf.

Deserts

A **desert** is a dry place. It gets lots of sunlight and little rain. Only a few kinds of plants and animals can live there.

desert

Desert Plants and Animals

Desert plants can hold water to use when they need it. Some, like the yucca, have thick leaves with a waxy coat. Others hold water in their thick stems.

cactus wren

yucca

beavertail cactus

Most deserts are hot. Desert animals have ways to stay cool and get water. Some, like the armadillo, stay in the shade. They look for food at night when it is cooler. Others, like the kangaroo rat, get water from their food.

■ **How do many of these animals stay cool?**

armadillo

rattlesnake

kangaroo rat

Think About It

1. What is a desert?
2. How do plants and animals live in a desert?

What Lives in a Rain Forest?

Investigate

Rain Forest Plants

You will need

seeds

2 wet cotton balls

film cans and lid with hole

plastic and rubber band

wet cotton ball

seeds

wet cotton ball

seeds

plastic

rubber band

1 Rain forest plants get little light. Make a model of a rain forest like this one. Close lid.

2 Plants in open areas get more light. Make a model of an open area.

3 Set both models in the sun for 5 days. Tell how the cotton changes.

Science Skill

To communicate how the forests grew, draw and share pictures of what you observed.

Rain Forests

A **rain forest** is wet all year. Most rain forests are warm, too. Rain and warm weather help trees and other plants grow. Animals use the plants to meet their needs.

rain forest

Rain Forest Animals and Plants

Animals live at different levels of the rain forest. Macaws live near the treetops. They find fruit to eat. Sloths hang from the middle of trees. They find shelter there and plants to eat.

macaw

three-toed sloths

orchid

Rain forest plants also live at different levels. Most grow from roots in the soil. Some, like the orchid, grow from roots halfway up trees. They get the light they need there.

bromeliad

■ **Where does this bromeliad live?**

Think About It

1. What is a rain forest?
2. How do plants and animals live in a rain forest?

What Lives in the Ocean?

Ocean Animals

You will need

ocean picture cards

1 Which ocean pictures show fish? Which show other animals?

2 Classify the animals. Put them in groups.

3 Share your groups. Talk about other ways to classify the animals.

Science Skill

When you classify the animals, you group them to show ways they are the same.

Oceans

An **ocean** is a large, deep body of salt water. Oceans cover three fourths of the Earth.

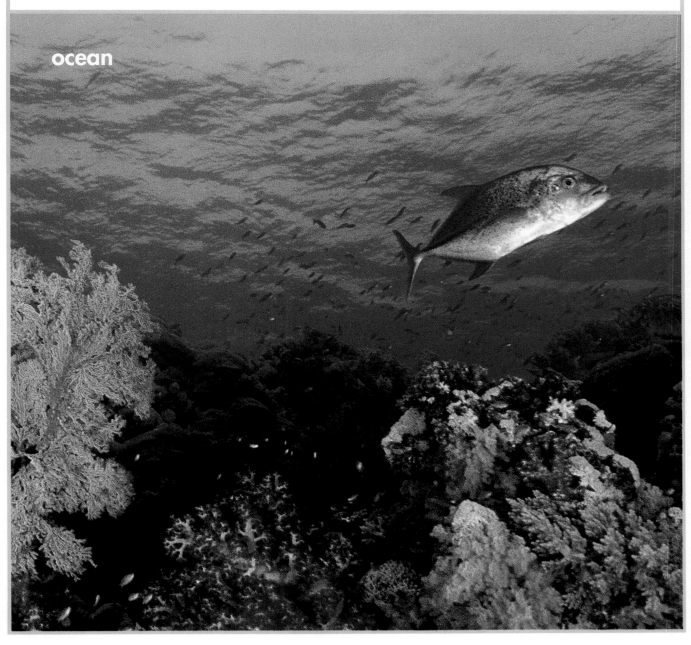

ocean

Ocean Plants and Animals

Some ocean plants are called **algae**. Many ocean animals use algae for food and shelter.

parrot fish

■ **What is the parrot fish using the algae for?**

bottle-nosed dolphin

green sea turtle

starfish

Ocean animals can find what they need in ocean waters. Dolphins' strong tails help them swim fast to catch fish.

Sea turtles use their flippers to swim and catch food.

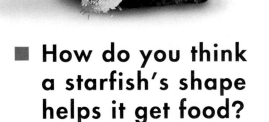
■ How do you think a starfish's shape helps it get food?

Think About It

1. What is an ocean?
2. How do ocean animals get what they need to live?

Math Link

Observe Leaf Patterns

You can find leaf patterns on a tree twig. A tree grows leaves the same way again and again. The leaves make a pattern.

Think and Do

Look at a tree twig with leaves. Observe how the leaves grow in a pattern. Draw a picture that shows the pattern.

A Scientist Investigates the Ocean

Sylvia Earle is a marine biologist, a scientist who studies life in the ocean. She dives deep to find out about ocean plants and animals. She also helps people learn about the ocean.

Think and Do

Choose a plant or an animal that lives in the ocean. Read books to learn more about it. Make a poster that tells about the plant or animal.

Tell What You Know

1. Tell about where each animal lives.

Vocabulary

Tell which picture goes with the word or words.

2. algae

3. rain forest

4. ocean

5. desert

6. forest

a.   b.   c.

d.   e.

Using Science Skills

7. Classify Read the clues. Name each plant or animal. Tell where it lives.

a. This plant has thorns that keep animals from eating it. It has a waxy coat to keep water in.

b. This animal has fins for swimming. It uses algae for food and shelter.

c. This plant lives halfway up on trees. It needs a warm, wet place.

8. Compare Look at the graph. Tell which place gets the most rain in a month.

How Much Rain Falls in a Month?	
Temperate Forest	⬇ ⬇ ⬇ ⬇ ⬇
Rain Forest	⬇ ⬇ ⬇ ⬇ ⬇ ⬇ ⬇ ⬇ ⬇ ⬇ ⬇ ⬇ ⬇ ⬇ ⬇
Desert	⬇

Each ⬇ equals 2 centimeters.

What Do Worms Need?

1. Put two kinds of soil and two worms in a covered box.

2. In two hours, check where the worms are.

3. What do the worms need? Talk about what you observe.

Make a Bird Feeder

1. Spread peanut butter on a pinecone.

2. Roll the pinecone in birdseed.

3. Hang the pinecone with string outdoors.

4. Observe birds that eat the seeds.

Rain Forest in a Jar

1. Put pebbles, soil, and plants in a jar.

2. Water the plants. Put the lid on the jar.

3. Put the jar where it gets light but not strong sun.

4. Wait one day. Observe. How is this like a rain forest?

Stalks That Store Water

1. Observe the stem pipes on a cut celery stalk.

2. Set the stalk in an empty cup. Wait until the celery droops.

3. Add cold water to the cup. Tell what happened and why.

stem pipes

Animals in Your Neighborhood

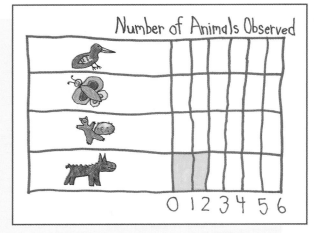

Number of Animals Observed

0 1 2 3 4 5 6

1. Take a walk with your class or with family members.

2. Count the animals in your neighborhood that are using plants.

3. Make a bar graph to show your information.

Animal Teeth

With a classmate or a family member, look for pictures of mammals eating other animals or plants. Decide if each mammal has flat teeth or sharp teeth. Sort your pictures into two groups.

Flat Teeth   Sharp Teeth

A Place to Live

Is a forest, a desert, a rain forest, or an ocean your favorite place to learn about? With a classmate or a family member, make a shoe-box display that shows plants and animals of your favorite place.

Camel in the Desert

Put your hand in a box of sand. Keep your fingers together and "walk" in the sand. Now spread your fingers and "walk." Which way is easier? Why?

WRITING

Collage What do plants or pets in a classroom need to live? Make a picture. Write your ideas.

READING

The Very Hungry Caterpillar **by Eric Carle** How does the hungry caterpillar use plants? Share your ideas.

COMPUTER CENTER
Visit *The Learning Site* at www.harcourtschool.com/ca

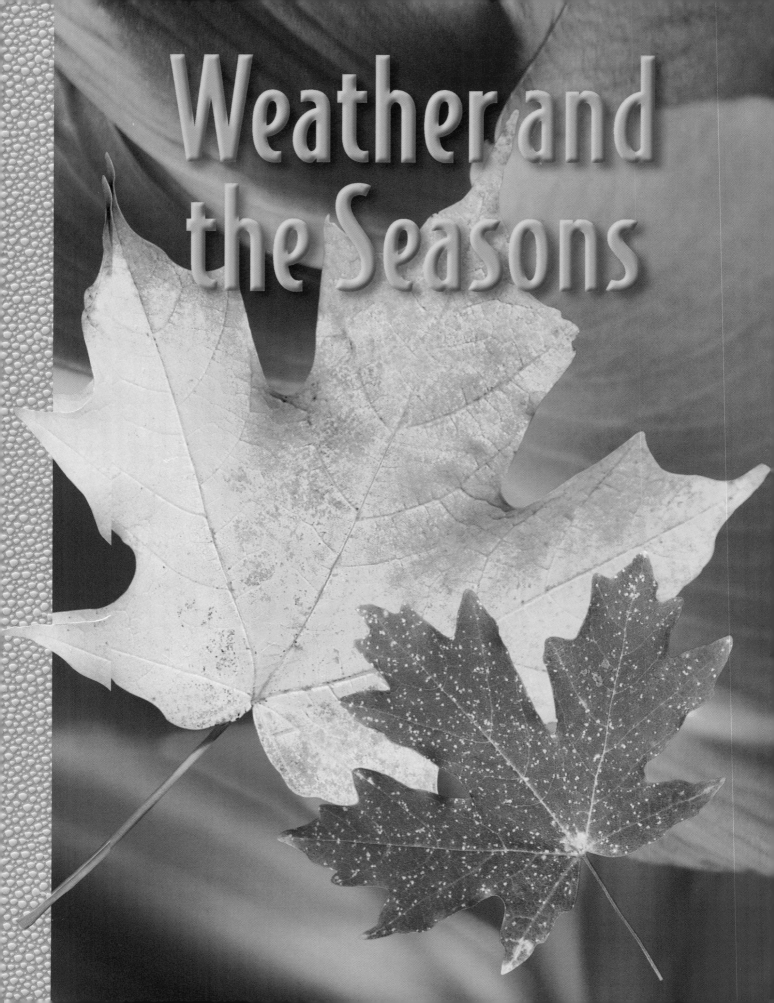

Weather and the Seasons

Weather and the Seasons

UNIT PROJECT

The Four Seasons
Make a mobile for each season. Show plants, animals, weather, and clothing.

Measuring Weather

Vocabulary

weather
temperature
thermometer
wind
water vapor
evaporate
condense
water cycle

Did You Know?
You don't have to have rainy **weather** to get lightning.

Did You Know?
A landsailer can go more than 100 miles an hour in the **wind**.

What Is Weather?

Weather Conditions

You will need

paper   markers

1 Observe the changes in weather.

2 Draw or write what you observe.

3 Compare observations with a classmate. Add your page to a class book.

Science Skill

When you compare the things you observed, tell how they are the same and different.

Weather

It may be hot or cold outside. It may be sunny, cloudy, or rainy. All these words tell about weather. The **weather** is what the air outside is like.

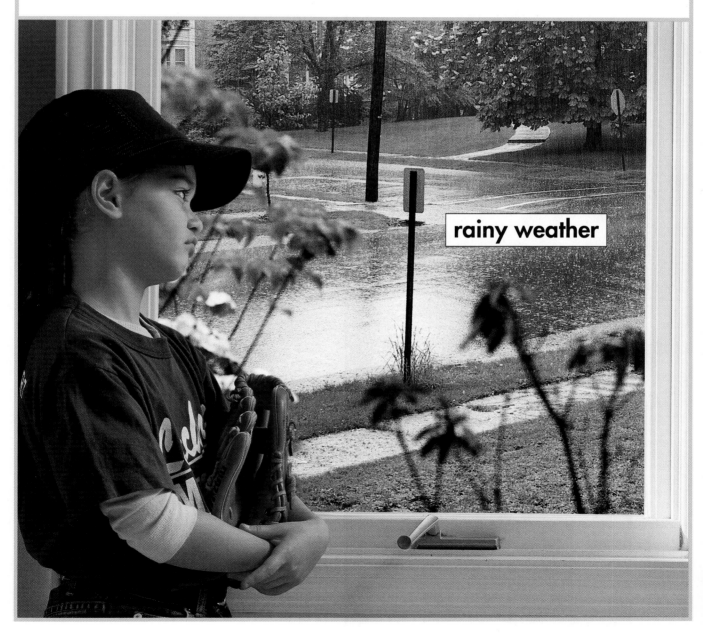

rainy weather

Different Kinds of Weather

When the air outside changes, the weather changes. The weather may be hot one day and cool the next.

One day may be cloudy and rainy. The next day may be clear and sunny. One day may be very windy. Another day may be calm.

■ **How are these kinds of weather different?**

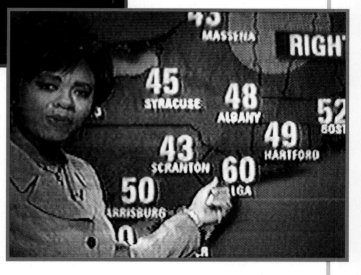

Meteorologist

People like to know what the weather will be. They check weather reports made by a meteorologist. A meteorologist is a scientist who studies weather.

Think About It

1. What is weather?

2. How can weather change from day to day?

What Is Temperature?

Measuring Air Temperature

You will need

thermometer

paper and pencil

red crayon

1 Draw and label two thermometers.

2 Measure and record the air temperature in the classroom.

3 Put the thermometer outside for 5 minutes. Measure and record the air temperature.

4 Compare the temperatures.

Science Skill

To measure temperature with a thermometer, read the number next to the top of the red line.

Temperature

The **temperature** is the measure of how hot or cold something is. Temperature is measured with a tool called a **thermometer**.

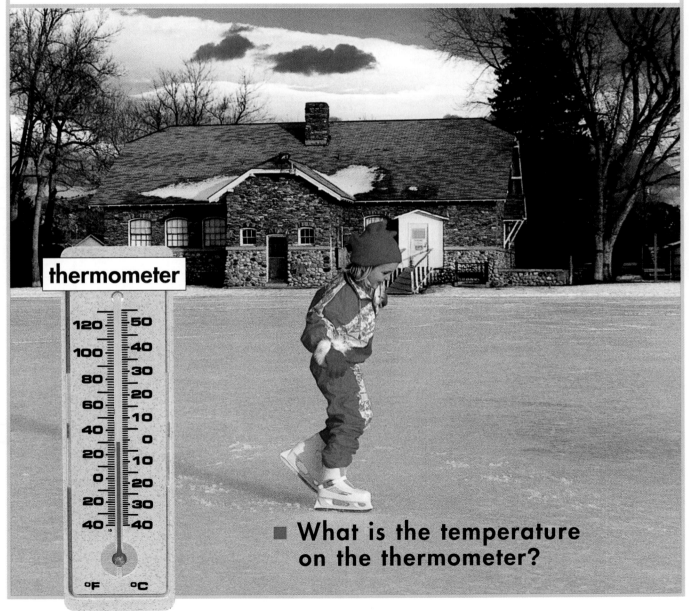

thermometer

■ **What is the temperature on the thermometer?**

Different Temperatures

The temperature of the air changes from day to day. It also changes as the seasons change. Sometimes it is so low that water freezes. Sometimes it is so high that an ice pop melts.

- **How does the temperature change in these pictures?**

Air temperature may also change during the day. In the daytime the sun warms the land, air, and water. The temperature goes up.

At night the sun does not warm the air. The temperature goes down, and the land, air, and water feel cooler.

daytime

early evening

■ **How are the temperatures different here? Why?**

Think About It

1. What is a thermometer? How do you use it?

2. What is temperature? How does it change?

What Is Wind?

Wind Direction

You will need

drinking
straw

round
toothpick

paper
triangle

tape

1 Make a wind vane. Poke the toothpick through the straw.

✂ **CAUTION** Be careful. Toothpicks are sharp.

2 Tape the triangle to the straw. Go outdoors. Hold up the toothpick.

3 Observe the wind's direction on two windy days.

Science Skill

To observe the wind's direction, check which way the triangle points.

Wind

Moving air is called **wind**. Wind can push things. It can push a sailboat across a lake or blow a wind vane.

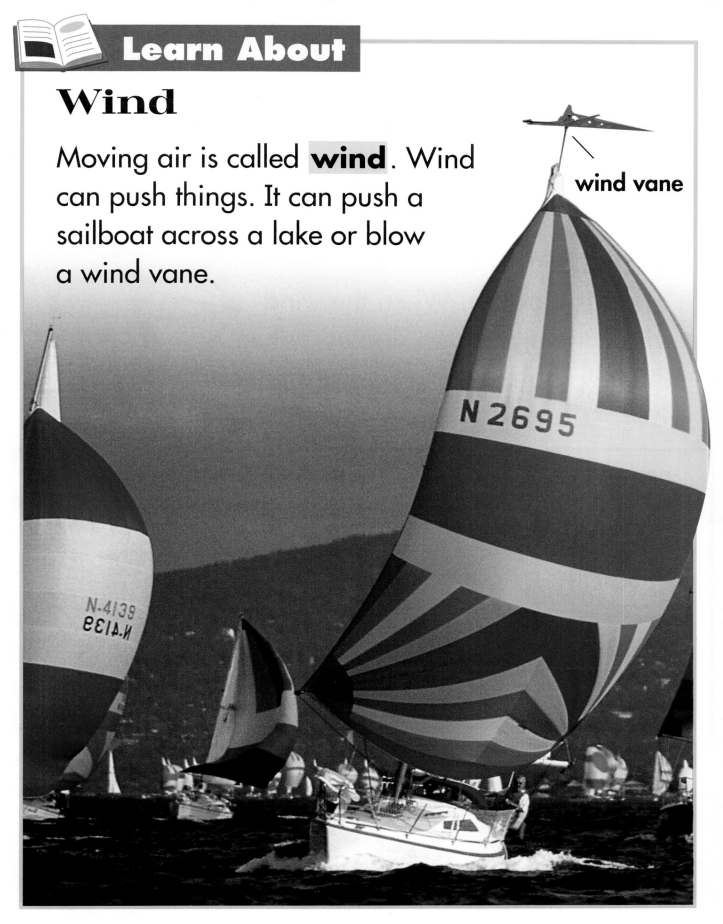

wind vane

N 2695

N-4139

Different Kinds of Wind

Sometimes the wind blows gently. Sometimes it blows hard.

A flag can show how hard the wind is blowing. When the wind blows gently, a flag ripples. When it blows hard, a flag flies straight out.

| no wind | light wind | medium wind | strong wind |

■ **How does a flag show how hard the wind is blowing?**

Strong wind turns windmills to make electricity. Sometimes wind can be too strong. The strong winds of a tornado can break up buildings.

Think About It

1. What is wind?
2. What are some different kinds of wind?

What Makes Clouds and Rain?

How Clouds Form

You will need

jar with lid

very warm water

ice cubes

1 Pour warm water into the jar. Wait. Pour out most of the water.

CAUTION Be careful. Water is hot!

2 Set the lid upside down on the jar. Observe the jar.

3 Put ice on the lid. Observe. Infer how clouds form.

Science Skill

To infer, first observe. Then think about what happened and draw a conclusion.

Clouds and Rain

Clouds are made up of many tiny drops of water. The drops may join and get heavier. When the drops get too heavy, they fall as rain.

The Water Cycle

Water moves from the Earth to the sky and back again in the **water cycle**.

2 Water vapor meets cooler air. It will then **condense**, or change into tiny drops of water. The drops form clouds.

1 The sun warms water and air. The water will **evaporate**, or change into water vapor.

Water vapor is water that you can not see in the air.

3 The water drops join and get heavier. They fall to Earth as rain, hail, sleet, or snow.

Think About It

1. How do clouds form?

2. How does rain form?

Math Link

Measure Air Temperature

Monday

Tuesday

In some places the air temperature changes a lot from day to day. In other places it changes only a little.

Temperature Changes	
Day of Week	Degrees Fahrenheit
Monday	60
Tuesday	40
Wednesday	

Think and Do

Use a thermometer. Measure and record the temperature each day. Tell about the temperature changes.

Language Arts Link

Weather Sayings

Long ago, sailors looked for patterns to predict the weather. This is one of their sayings.

Red sky at night,
Sailors' delight.
Red sky at morning,
Sailors take warning.

Sailors observed that a red sunset often comes before a sunny day. A red sunrise often comes before a rainy day.

Think and Do

Observe the weather for a week. Look for patterns. Make up a weather saying about a pattern you observe.

Tell What You Know

1. Tell what you know about the diagram. Use the words *water cycle, water vapor, evaporate,* and *condense.*

Vocabulary

Use each word to tell about the picture.

weather

temperature

4.

thermometer

5.

wind

Using Science Skills

6. Compare Make a chart about the weather. Observe and compare the weather in the morning and in the afternoon. Tell about the changes.

Today's Weather		
	Morning	Afternoon
How It Looks		
How It Sounds		
How It Feels		
How It Smells		

7. Observe Collect or draw pictures of clouds. Write a label for each picture.

Write a sentence that tells what each cloud looks like. Tell what weather you might have with that cloud.

The Seasons

Vocabulary

season

spring

summer

fall

winter

Did You Know?
Many parts of the world have four seasons, but the tropical rain forest only has one **season**.

Did You Know?
When it is **summer** in North America, it is **winter** in South America.

What Is Spring?

What Helps Seeds Sprout

You will need

4 bean seeds   **2 cups**   **mist bottle**   **paper towels**   **hand lens**

1 Put a damp paper towel in each cup. Add two seeds to each. Label the cups *winter* and *spring*.

2 Put the *winter* cup in a cold, dark place. Put the *spring* cup in a warm, dark place.

3 Observe the seeds with the hand lens three days later. What can you infer?

Science Skill
To infer, first observe, and then think about what you see.

Spring

Spring is the season that follows winter. A **season** is a time of year. In spring, there are more hours of daylight. The air gets warmer. Spring rains fall.

spring   summer   fall   winter

Plants and Animals in Spring

More daylight, warmer air, and spring rains help plants start growing. For farmers, spring is a good time to plant seeds.

■ How does spring help these plants start growing?

■ **Which are the young animals?**

Many animals give birth to their young in spring. Birds build nests and lay eggs. Lambs and other animals are born. The growing plants are food for many young animals.

Think About It

1. What is a season?
2. What is spring?

What Is Summer?

Investigate

Colors That Can Keep You Cool

You will need

4 thermometers

4 colors of paper

stapler

clock

1 Fold and staple 4 color sheets of paper to make sleeves. Put a thermometer in each. Place in the sun.

2 Record the starting temperatures for each.

3 Wait 30 minutes. Record the temperatures again. Order from hottest to coolest.

Science Skill

To put the colors in order, start with the one with the hottest temperature. End with the coolest.

Summer

Summer is the season that follows spring. Summer has the most hours of daylight of any season. In many places the air gets hot.

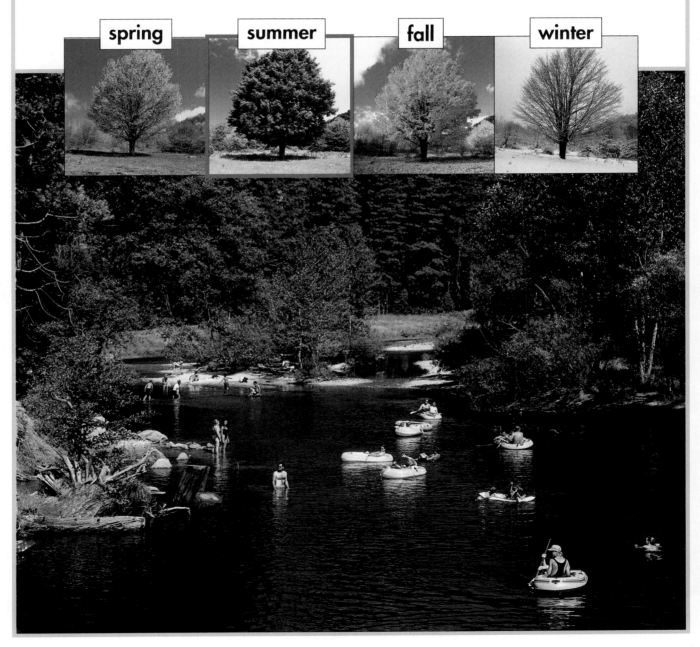

spring summer fall winter

Plants and Animals in Summer

In summer, lots of sunlight helps plants grow leaves and flowers. Soon fruits begin to form and grow.

■ **What do these plants get in summer that helps them make fruit?**

In summer, young animals eat and grow. Young horses, called foals, become strong and fast.

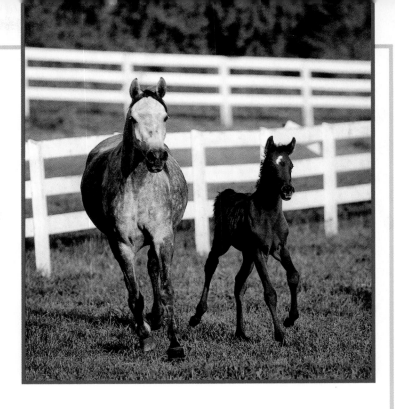

Young birds lose their first feathers. They begin to look like adults.

Think About It

1. What is summer?
2. How is summer different from spring?

What Is Fall?

Investigate

Storing Apples

You will need

apple rings   string   plastic bag   paper and pencil

1 Put some apple rings in the plastic bag. Store them on a shelf.

2 Hang the other apple rings on string. Don't let them touch.

3 Predict and record what will happen.

4 Wait one week. Record.

Science Skill

To predict which way to store apple rings is better, use what you know about food. Then decide.

Fall

The season that follows summer is **fall**. In fall, there are fewer hours of daylight. The air grows cool. In some places, leaves change colors and drop to the ground.

spring   summer   fall   winter

Plants and Animals in Fall

In fall, plants get less sunlight and stop growing bigger. They make seeds that will sprout next spring. Fruits and vegetables are ready to be picked.

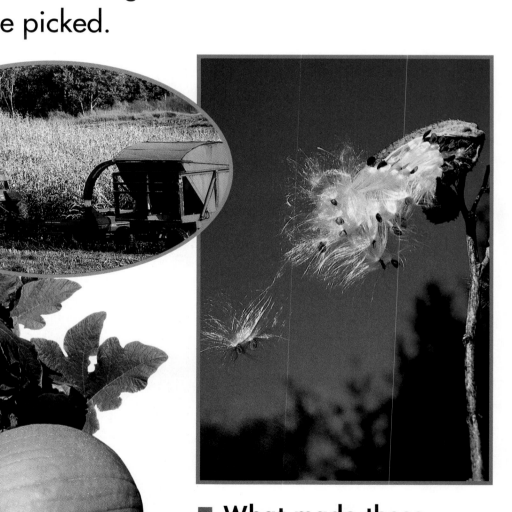

■ **What made these plants stop growing bigger?**

When plants stop growing, animals have less food. Some animals move to places where there is more food. Others store food so they have something to eat in winter.

Think About It

1. What is fall?
2. How is fall different from summer?

What Is Winter?

Keeping Warm in Cold Weather

You will need

plastic bag

container of
ice water

things to keep
your hand warm

1 Put your hand in the bag. Then put your hand in the ice water. Does the bag keep your hand warm?

2 What could you put in the bag to keep your hand warm? Choose some things to try.

3 Investigate your ideas by trying them. Which one works best?

Science Skill

To **investigate** how to keep your hand warm, try out each of your ideas.

Winter

Winter is the season that follows fall. There are fewer hours of daylight than in fall. In many places the air gets cold and snow falls.

spring

summer

fall

winter

Plants and Animals in Winter

In winter, days do not have many hours of sunlight. The branches of many trees and bushes are bare.

Some plants are resting. Some plants that made seeds are now dead.

Where winters are cold, animals can not find much food. Some eat food they stored in fall.

■ **How do these animals meet their needs for food in winter?**

Think About It

1. What is winter?

2. What are some ways animals live in winter?

Art Link

A Photographer Observes the Seasons

Ansel Adams was a photographer. Each season, he took pictures of his favorite places. His photographs help us see the beauty of the seasons.

fall

winter

Think and Do

Think of your favorite place. Draw pictures to show it in different seasons. Label each picture with the season it shows.

Math Link

Read a Graph

In a part of northern California, some seasons are wet and some are dry. This graph shows about how many inches or centimeters of rain fall in each season.

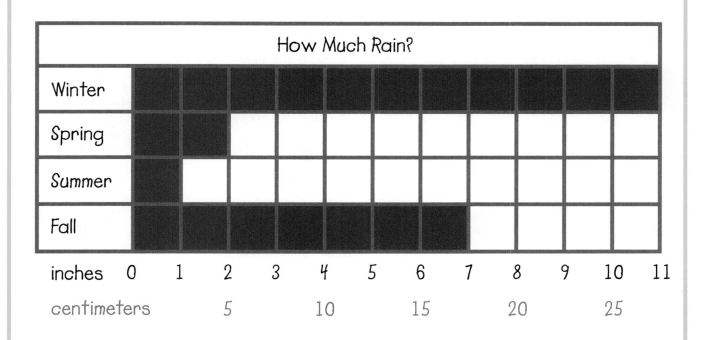

How Much Rain?											
Winter											
Spring											
Summer											
Fall											

inches 0 1 2 3 4 5 6 7 8 9 10 11

centimeters 5 10 15 20 25

Think and Do

Look at the bar graph. Which season is the wettest in northern California? Which is the driest?

Tell What You Know

1. Tell what you know about the pictures. Use the word *spring*, *summer*, *fall*, or *winter* to tell about each one.

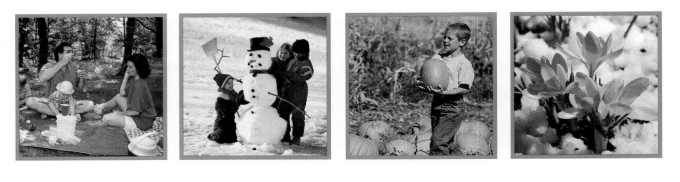

Vocabulary

Use each word to tell about the picture.

season

spring

summer

fall

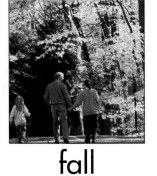

winter

Using Science Skills

7. **Order** Use four sheets of paper. On each, write the name of one of the seasons. Then draw the clothes you would wear. Put your sheets in order, beginning with summer.

8. **Predict and Investigate** Look at the colors of these shirts. Predict which color will stay the coolest in hot sun. Write your prediction. Use any color paper to investigate your idea.

Make a Sail for a Car

Put a paper sail on a toy car. Blow on the sail to make the car move. What could you do to make a better sail? Try your ideas.

Investigate Water Vapor

1. With an adult present, blow into a small plastic bag.

2. Observe the water drops inside. They come from the water vapor in your breath.

3. Put the bag in a freezer for five minutes. Tell what happens.

4. Put the bag in the sun for five minutes. Tell what happens.

Make a Four Seasons Poster

Fold a big sheet of paper into four parts. Label each part for a different season. Add pictures of things you like to do in each season. Talk about your poster.

Find Seasons in a Closet

What clothes do people wear at different times of the year where you live? Brainstorm ideas. Write a list that shows at least two things for each season.

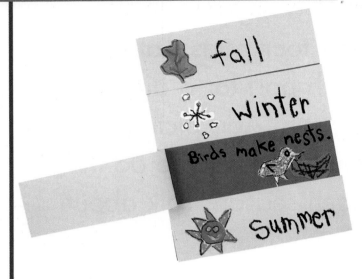

WRITING

Flap Facts Make a flap book about the seasons. Under each flap, tell one thing about that season.

READING

Animal Seasons
by Brian Wildsmith
Read about ways plants and animals change with the seasons. Talk about how the weather changes.

 COMPUTER CENTER
Visit *The Learning Site* at
www.harcourtschool.com/ca

Matter and
Energy

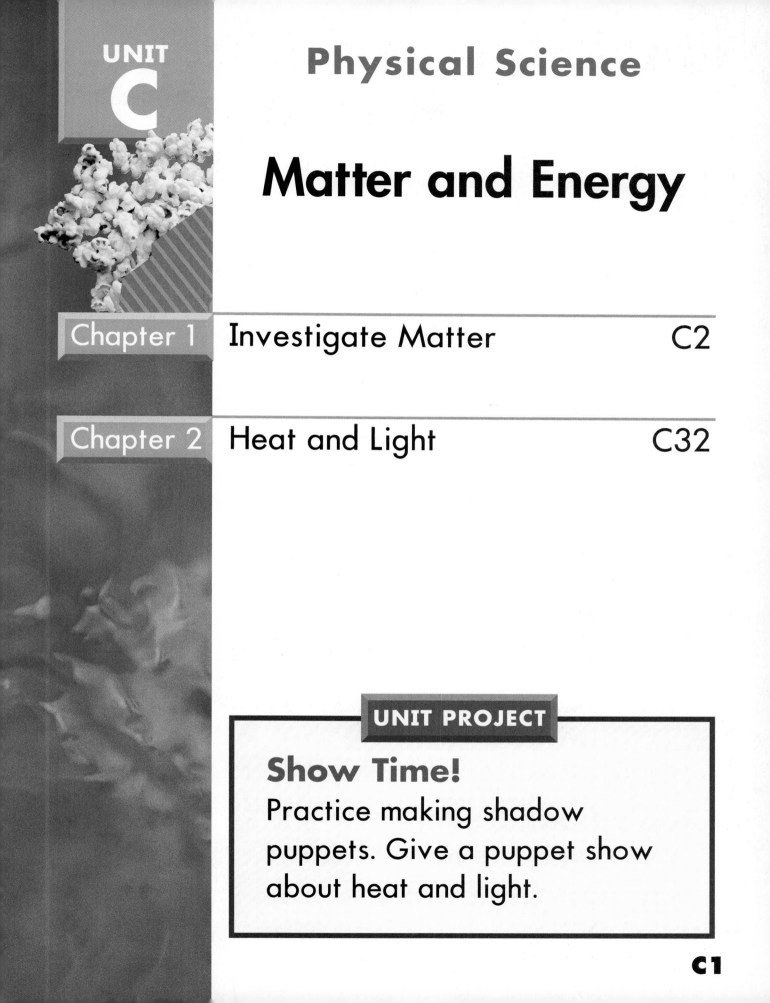

UNIT
C

Physical Science

Matter and Energy

UNIT PROJECT

Show Time!
Practice making shadow puppets. Give a puppet show about heat and light.

C1

Investigate Matter

Vocabulary

solid
matter
liquid
float
sink
gas
change
mechanic

Did You Know?
Boats **float** higher
in salt water than
they do in fresh water.

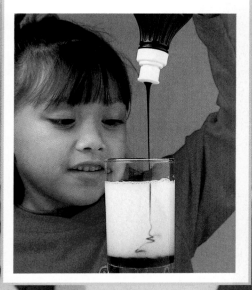

What Can We Observe About Solids?

Solid Objects

You will need

objects

paper and pencil

1 Observe each object.

2 Compare the sizes, shapes, and colors of the objects.

3 Think of three ways to classify the objects. Draw or write them on your paper.

Science Skill
To classify the objects, find ways they are the same and group them.

Matter and Solids

Everything around you is **matter**.
Toys and blocks are matter. You are, too!

■ **What matter do you see?**

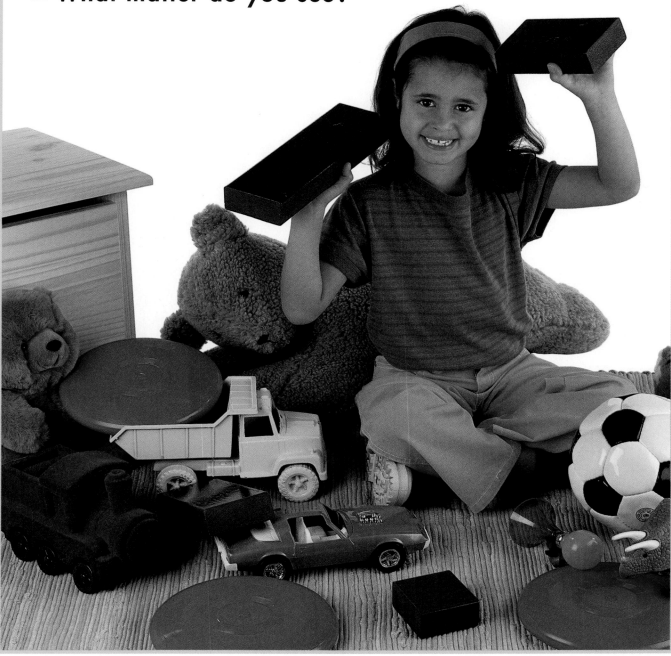

Observing Solids

Some matter is solid. A **solid** is matter that keeps its shape. It keeps its shape even when you move it.

■ **How do you know these toys are solids?**

Liquids

Matter that flows is called a **liquid**. A liquid does not have a shape of its own. It takes the shape of the container you pour it into.

Observing Liquids

Some liquids, like water, are thin. Others are thick. Some liquids mix with water. Some, such as oil, do not mix with water.

Thin liquids flow quickly. Thick liquids flow slowly. This pan has dish soap, honey, and juice running down it.

Which Liquid Flows Fastest?	
Liquid	Time
dish soap	9 seconds
honey	47 seconds
juice	1 second

■ **Read the chart. Which liquid flows fastest?**

Think About It

1. What is a liquid?

2. What can we observe about liquids?

What Objects Sink or Float?

 Investigate

Shapes That Sink or Float

You will need

ball of clay

aquarium with water

paper and pencil

1 Gather data about shapes that sink or float. Put the clay ball in the water.

2 Record data about what happens.

3 Make the clay into different shapes. Do they sink or float? Record.

Science Skill

When you gather data, you observe things. When you record data, you write and draw what you observe.

Objects That Sink or Float

Some objects **float**, or stay on top of a liquid. Others **sink**, or drop to the bottom of a liquid. You can change the shape of some objects to make them float or sink.

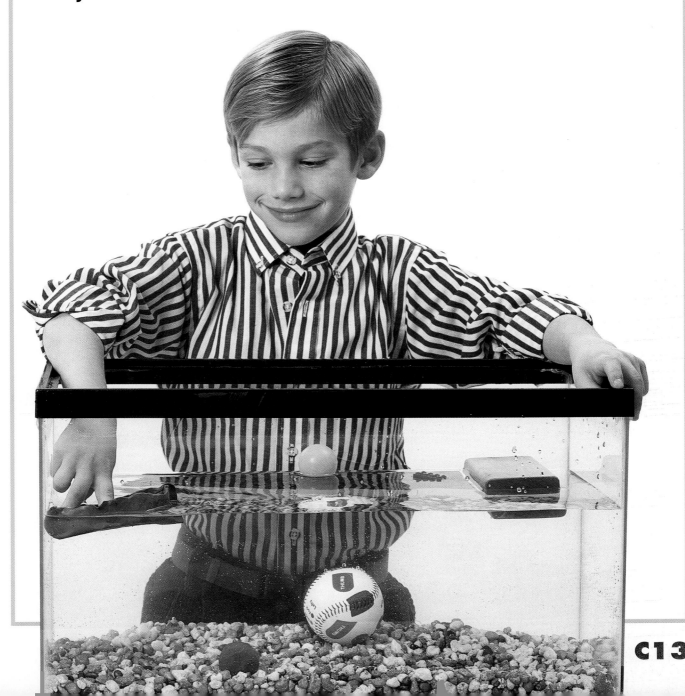

Floaters and Sinkers

You can not always guess which objects will float. You must test them to find out.

You can group objects as floaters or sinkers. What objects here would you put into these two groups? Why?

Think About It

1. What do *float* and *sink* mean?
2. What helps an object sink or float?

What Can We Observe About Gases?

Air in a Bottle

You will need

balloon

plastic soft drink bottle

1 Squeeze the bottle to observe the air in it. Blow up the balloon. Feel the air come out.

2 Put the balloon in the bottle. Pull the end over the top.

3 Try to blow up the balloon. What else is in the bottle? Draw a conclusion.

Science Skill

To draw a conclusion about what happened, think about what you observed.

Gases

Gases are matter. A **gas** does not have a shape of its own. It spreads out to fill its container and take its shape.

Observing Gases

Gases are all around you. Air is made up of different gases. You can not see most gases, but you can see what they do.

A gas fills up the space inside a balloon. A fan makes air blow your hair.

Some gases, like the gas in this soft drink, can mix with water. You can see bubbles in the soft drink as the gas comes out.

Like all matter, gases take up space. Air takes up space in this cup, so no water can come in.

Think About It

1. What are gases?
2. What can we observe about gases?

How Can We Change Objects?

Changing Paper

You will need

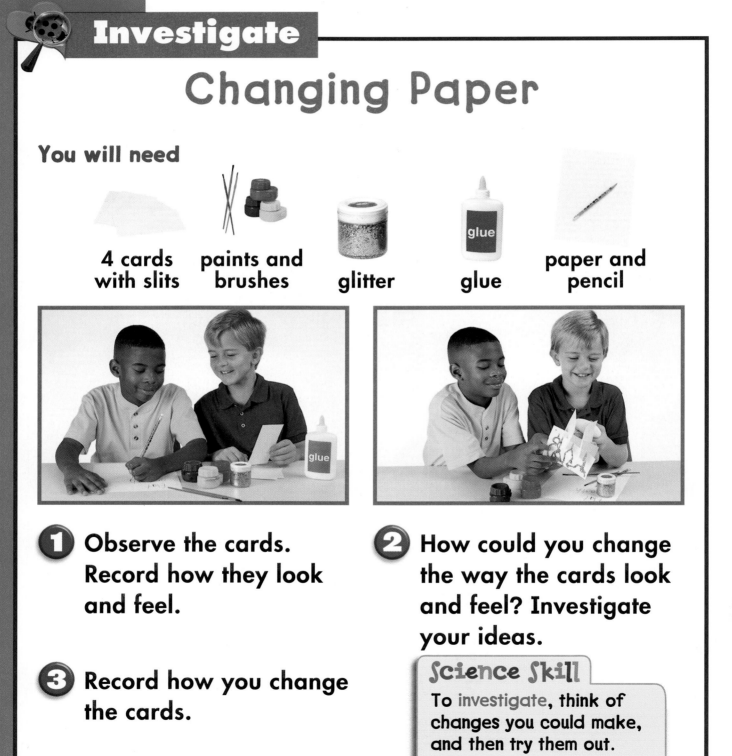

4 cards with slits | paints and brushes | glitter | glue | paper and pencil

1 Observe the cards. Record how they look and feel.

2 How could you change the way the cards look and feel? Investigate your ideas.

3 Record how you change the cards.

Science Skill

To investigate, think of changes you could make, and then try them out.

Changing Objects

You can **change** objects, or make them different. You can change their shape, size, color, or texture.

Observing Changes

You can change objects in different ways. You can roll or bend some objects to change their shape.

■ **How can you change clay from a lump into coils that stack?**

You can change some liquids by cooling or freezing them. Freezing changes fruit juice into a frozen ice pop.

You can change an object by mixing it with other things. You might make a rock animal for fun. It might be a mix of the rock, paint, and other things.

■ **How did someone change this rock to look like a spider?**

Think About It

1. What are some things you can change about objects?
2. What are three things you can do to objects to change them?

What Happens When Objects Are Taken Apart?

Investigate

Wheels and an Axle

You will need

2 paper plates

ballpoint pen

1 Make a model of two wheels and an axle. Poke the pen through the plates. Do the plate wheels roll?

 CAUTION Be careful. The pen point is sharp!

2 Take apart the wheels and axle. Do the wheels roll? Draw a conclusion.

Objects and Their Parts

Many objects are made of parts.
The parts work together to make the
objects work. Without all their parts,
many objects will not work.

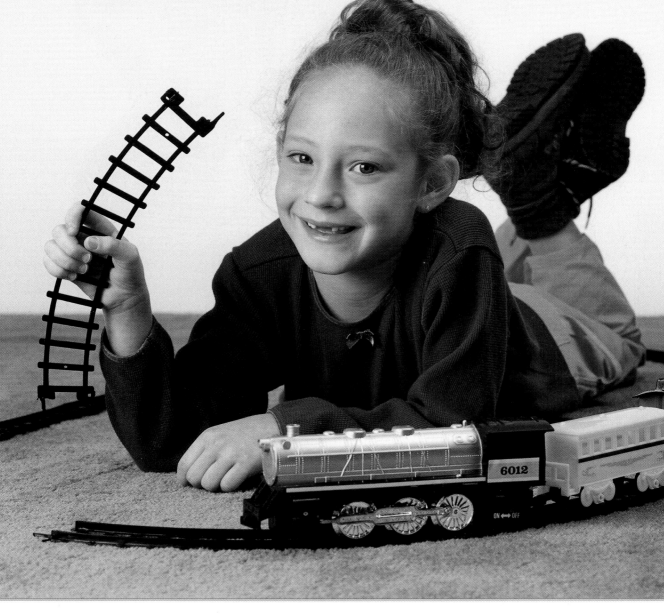

How Parts Work Together

A camera must have film to work. Without film, you can not take photographs. A plane must have fuel to fly. Without fuel, the plane's engine will not run.

Sometimes a car does not work the way it should. A **mechanic** can fix a broken part or put in a new one. Then the car will work the way it should again.

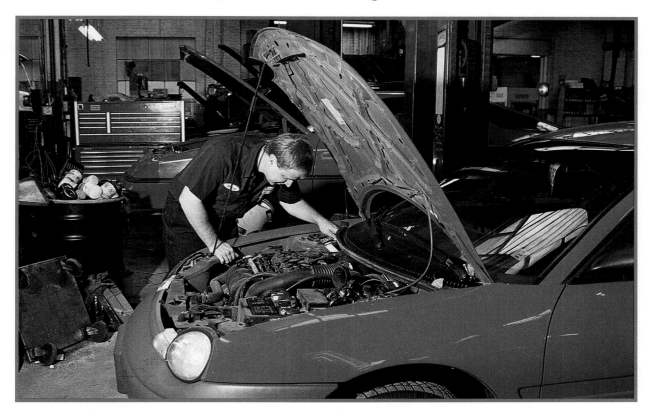

Think About It

1. What happens when objects do not have all their parts?

2. What does a mechanic do if a car part is broken?

Art Link

Mixing Objects to Make Art

A Spanish artist named Pablo Picasso made this sculpture. He used two everyday objects to show something new. Look at the bicycle seat and handlebars.

■ **How does this art look like a bull's head?**

Bull's Head by Pablo Picasso

Think and Do

Choose two or three objects in your classroom. Plan a way to put them together to show something new. Then follow your plan.

How Much Can Ships Carry?

Big ships can carry heavy cargo. On the left you see a ship with no cargo. The red line shows that it is floating high in the water. On the right you see a ship loaded with cargo. You can not see the red line. The ship is floating lower in the water.

Think and Do

Make a foil boat. Put it in the water. Slowly put pennies in your boat. How many pennies can it carry without sinking?

Tell What You Know

1. Use the word *solid, liquid,* or *gas* to tell about each picture.

Vocabulary

Use each word to tell about the picture.

2.

matter

3.

float

4.

sink

5.

change

6.

mechanic

Using Science Skills

7. Gather and Record Data
Make a chart to gather and record data about liquids. Put one drop of water and one drop of oil on wax paper.

Liquids				
	Makes a Round Drop	Makes a Flat Drop	Can Be Dragged	Can Not Be Dragged
Water				
Oil				

Observe each drop. Use a toothpick to drag each one. Try other liquids and add them to the chart.

8. Draw a Conclusion Think about what makes these cars roll. Draw a conclusion about why one car rolled farther.

Heat and Light

Vocabulary

heat
melt
prism
refract
reflect

Did You Know?
The blue part of
a flame gives off
the most **heat**.

Did You Know? Your hand gives off enough heat to **melt** some solids.

What Is Heat?

Investigate

What Heat Does to Water

You will need

2 cups
with water

2
thermometers

paper and
pencil

clock

1 Measure the temperature of the water in each cup.

2 Make a chart. Write a number to show each temperature.

3 Wait 10 minutes. Read and record each temperature.

4 Draw a conclusion.

Science Skill
Use numbers to tell what you found out. Compare the numbers. Draw a conclusion.

Heat

Heat can make things warmer. The sun gives off heat. The sun's heat warms the Earth's land, air, and water.

Other Things That Give Off Heat

Fire also gives off heat. Heat from a fire warms the people sitting around it.

■ **How is the fire being used in this picture?**

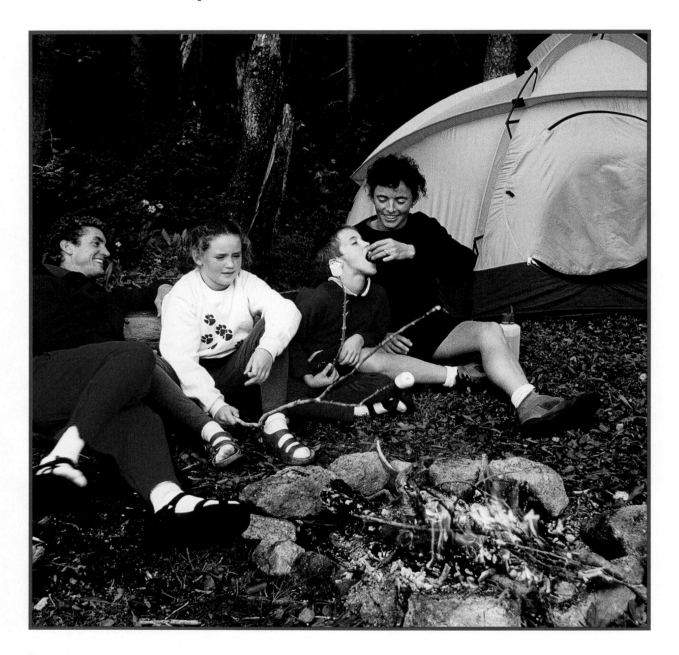

Rubbing Makes Heat

Almost anything gives off heat if you rub it. Try rubbing your hands together. Can you feel the heat they give off?

■ **What is this boy doing to make heat?**

Think About It

1. What does heat do?
2. What are some things that give off heat?

How Does Heat Change Matter?

How Heat Changes Water

You will need

food coloring

hot water in a bowl

cold water in a bowl

paper and pencil

1 Gather data about how heat changes water. Put a drop of food coloring in cold water. Record.

2 Put a drop of food coloring in hot water. Record.

 CAUTION Be careful. Hot!

3 How did heat change the water? Tell what you found out.

Science Skill

To gather data about something, observe it. Then draw or write to record your observations.

How Heat Changes Matter

Heat changes matter. It makes a solid melt and a liquid evaporate. It makes a gas spread out.

■ **How is the sun's heat changing this snowperson?**

What Heat Does to Matter

You can observe what heat does to matter. You can heat solids such as ice or sugar to melt them. When solids **melt**, they turn into liquids.

You can heat a liquid, such as soup. Some of it will evaporate, or change to a gas.

■ **What does heat do to these solids and liquids?**

You can heat a gas, such as air.
Hot air spreads out to fill this balloon.

Think About It

1. How does heat change a solid like ice?
2. How does heat change liquids and gases?

What Is Light?

Light and Color

You will need

prism

objects

paper and pencil

crayons or markers

flashlight

1 Shine a light. Look at objects through the prism.

2 Draw a picture of what you observe. Label it with the colors you observe.

3 Use your picture to communicate what you observed.

Science Skill

To communicate, use the labeled picture to talk about what you observed.

Light

Light lets us see. The sun gives off light as well as heat. The sun's light helps us see what is around us.

Other Things That Give Off Light

Many things besides the sun give off both light and heat. We can use their light to see when there is no sunlight.

■ **What are some things that give off both light and heat?**

Light and Color

Light is made of colors. You can see the colors when light passes through a prism. A **prism** is any clear object that breaks light into colors.

prism

Think About It

1. What does light do?

2. When can you see the colors light is made of?

What Can Light Do?

Making Light Bounce

You will need

flashlight with battery

index card in clay

mirror

1 Turn the flashlight on. Observe the light.

2 Put the mirror in front of the light. Move the mirror. Observe.

3 Investigate this problem. How can you make light shine on the card without moving the card?

Science Skill

To investigate a problem, you plan and try different ideas.

How Light Moves

Light moves in a straight line until it hits a solid or a liquid. Dust in the air helps us see light's straight lines.

What Light Can Do

When light hits something solid, it **reflects**, or bounces off in a new direction.

Light reflecting off a cat lets us see the cat. The cat's shadow shows where the cat blocks the light.

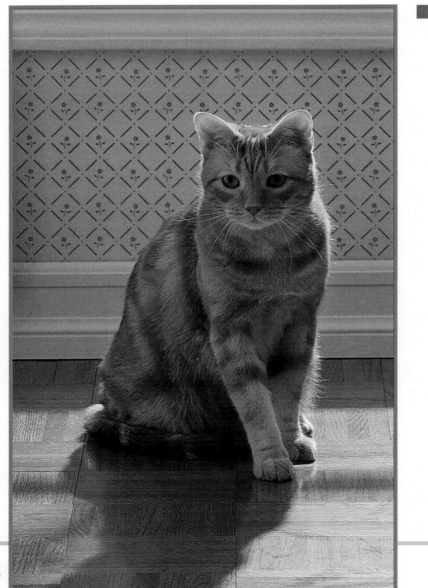

■ **What makes the cat's shadow?**

Light passes through water as well as air. Light may bend, or **refract** , where water and air meet. An object that is partly in water may look bent.

■ **What happens to light when it hits a mirror?**

Think About It

1. In what way does light move?

2. What can light do?

A Hot Air Balloonist Explores

Jetta Schantz flies hot air balloons. To go up, she heats the air in her balloon. The hot air in it spreads out and gets lighter. The cool air pushes it up and lifts the balloon.

Think and Do

Observe how hot air spreads out. Blow up a balloon about halfway, and tie it. Use a string to measure around it. Hold the balloon in hot water for a few minutes. Measure again.

Math Link

Measure Shadows

Children in many places have fun with shadows. Children in Indonesia make deer shadow puppets. They sing songs about what their puppets do.

With a partner, make shadow puppets on paper. How can you make them smaller or larger? Trace two shadows. Measure them with paper clips. Find the difference between the two.

Tell What You Know

1. Use the word *light* or *heat* to tell about each picture.

Tell which picture goes with each word.

2. prism

3. refract

4. melt

5. reflect

a.

b.

c.

d.

Using Science Skills

6. Gather Data Does a foam cup or a metal cup keep cocoa hotter over time? Gather your own data, or read the data in the chart. Use the data to decide which cup to use.

Which Cup Keeps Cocoa Hotter?			
Kind of Cup	Temperature at Start	After 5 Minutes	After 10 Minutes
Foam Cup	55 degrees Celsius	49 degrees Celsius	47 degrees Celsius
Metal Cup	55 degrees Celsius	47 degrees Celsius	43 degrees Celsius

7. Use Numbers Tape two mirrors together. Put a small object between them. Count how many times you see the object. Then move the mirrors. Make them show the object only once.

Activities
for Home or School

Make Juice Bars

Change liquid juice into a solid by making juice pops.

1. Have a family member help you pour fruit juice into an ice cube tray.

2. Put a toothpick into each part of the tray. *Be careful. Toothpicks are sharp.*

3. Cool them until frozen, and eat.

Floating Drops

1. Fill jar with salad oil.

2. Put two or three drops of food coloring into the oil. Put the lid on the jar.

3. Tip the jar. What happens to the colored drops? Talk about what floats and why.

Be a Shadow Tracker

1. In the morning, put a sheet of paper by a sunny window.

2. Put a stick in a ball of clay on the paper. Trace the stick's shadow. Write the time.

3. Trace the shadow and write the time again two more times that day.

4. Tell what happens to the shadow.

What Keeps Cold In?

1. Put one ice cube in a foam cup. Put another foam cup on top of that cup.

2. Do the same thing using two clear plastic cups.

3. Put both sets of cups in the sun.

4. Observe the ice cubes in one hour. Which cups would you use to keep a drink cold?

Water is a liquid.

WRITING

Tab Book On separate sheets of paper, write about solids, liquids, and gases. Add a label to each page. Put your pages together to make a book.

READING

Day Light, Night Light by Franklyn M. Branley Read about different places light comes from. Find the page that shows heat about to change a solid.

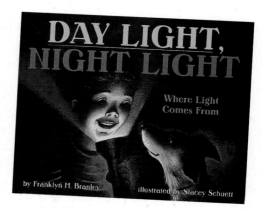

COMPUTER CENTER

Visit *The Learning Site* at www.harcourtschool.com/ca

Extension Chapters

California Science Standards

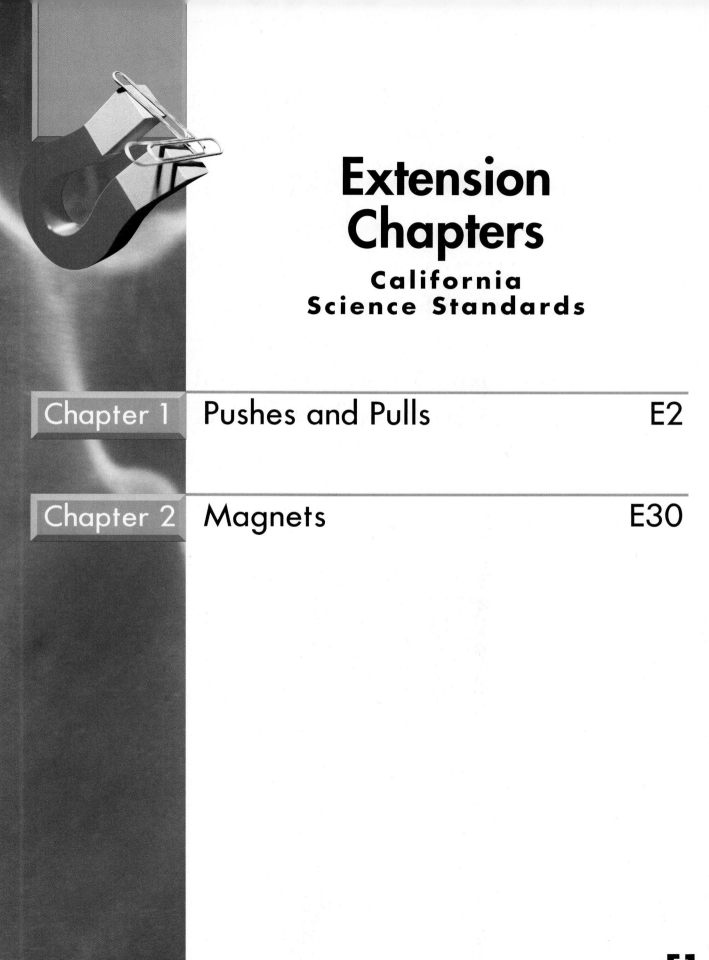

Extension Chapters

California
Science Standards

CHAPTER

1

Pushes and Pulls

Vocabulary

force
push
pull
zigzag
motion
surface
friction
wheel

Did You Know?
Tree roots can
push a rock when
they grow.

Did You Know?

The golden wheel spider can roll like a **wheel**.

What Makes Things Move?

Investigate

Pushes and Pulls

You will need

small block

things to make
the block move

paper
and pencil

1 What could you do to push or pull the block?

2 Write a plan to investigate your ideas. Then follow your plan.

3 Tell what you used to move the block. Use the word *push* or *pull*.

Science Skill

You investigate by thinking of ideas and trying them out.

Making Things Move

A **force** is a push or a pull. When you **push** something, you press it away. When you **pull** something, you tug it closer.

push

pull

Pushes and Pulls

Pushes and pulls make things move or stop moving. A tow truck pulls a car to the repair shop. A player pushes with a glove to stop a moving ball.

■ **Would the player use a push or a pull to throw the ball?**

A push or a pull can make something change direction. When you kick a ball, you are using a push. First the ball rolls to you. Your push makes it change direction. Then it moves away from you.

■ **What will the ball do when the player kicks it?**

Think About It

1. What is a force?

2. What can pushes and pulls do?

What Are Some Ways Things Move?

Moving Objects

You will need

objects

paper and pencil

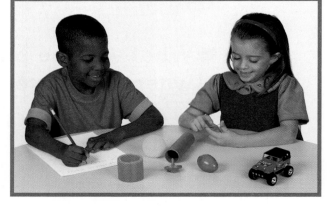

1 Observe and record how each object moves when you push or pull it.

2 Group objects that move the same way. Write how you grouped them.

Science Skill

To group the objects, put those that move in the same way together.

Ways Things Move

Pushes and pulls make things move in different ways. Tell what you know about how these rides move.

Telling How Things Move

There are different ways to tell how things move. One way is by the path they make. A car moves in a straight path. A skier may **zigzag**, or make sharp turns back and forth.

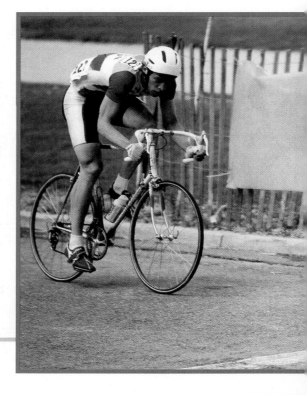

Another way to tell how things move is by their speed. Two bikers may start at the same time. If one moves ahead, he or she is moving faster.

Some things move the same way over and over. A top spins round and round. A swing moves back and forth.

■ **What kind of force keeps a swing moving?**

Think About It

1. What are some ways things move?
2. How can you tell if one thing is moving faster than another?

Why Do Things Move the Way They Do?

Investigate

Predicting Motion

You will need

ramp

plastic ball

tape

block

1 Set up the ramp. Predict where the ball will stop. Mark that place with tape.

2 Let the ball roll down the ramp. Was your prediction right?

3 Now put the block where the ball will hit it. Do Step 2 again.

Science Skill

To predict where the ball will stop, think about how a ball rolls and bounces.

Why Things Move the Way They Do

Moving from one place to another is **motion**. You can observe the motion of an object. This will help you predict where it will move next.

Changing Motion

A push or pull can change the motion of something. A hockey puck moves straight ahead unless something changes its motion.

Different kinds of pushes change how far the puck moves. A hard push moves the puck far. A gentle push moves it only a short way.

■ **What kind of push should the player use to move the puck a short way?**

Changing Direction

A force can change the direction in which an object moves. A ball will roll in one direction until something pushes it and makes it change.

■ **What does the paddle do to the ball in table tennis?**

Bumps are the pushes that change the direction of bumper boats. When you bump your boat against another boat, your boat bounces back.

Think About It

1. What is motion?
2. What can change the motion of something?

How Do Objects Move on Surfaces?

Investigate

Smooth and Rough Surfaces

You will need

 ramp

toy truck

meterstick

 paper and pencil

1 Set up a ramp on a smooth surface. Let the truck roll down.

2 Measure how far it rolls. Record the number. Do the same on a rough surface.

3 On which surface does the truck roll farther? Use your numbers to tell.

Science Skill
Measure how far the truck rolls from the end of the ramp to where the truck stops.

Different Surfaces

A **surface** is the top or outside of something. This floor has both a smooth surface and a rough surface. The truck moves in a different way on each surface.

More Friction, Less Friction

When two surfaces rub together, they make friction. **Friction** is a force that makes it harder to move things.

A rough surface makes more friction than a smooth one. On a rough road, a bike is harder to move. You have to push harder on the pedals.

■ **What surfaces rub together when you ride a bike over a road?**

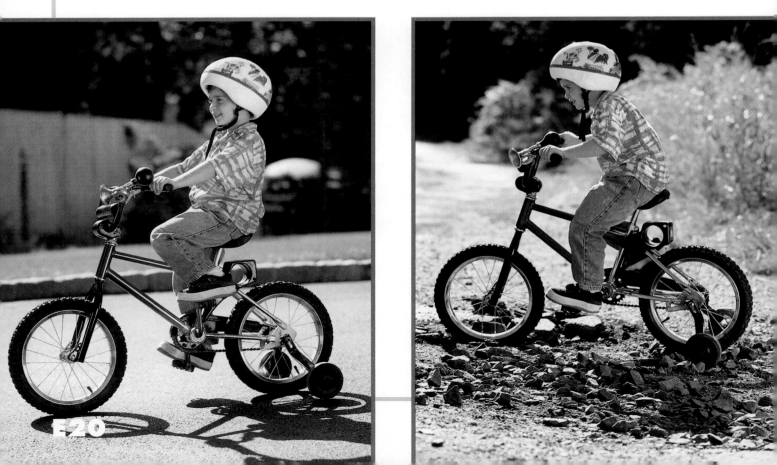

You can change how much friction a surface makes. If you cover a surface with something wet, it makes less friction. If you cover a surface with something rough, it makes more friction.

Think About It

1. What is friction?
2. What kind of surface makes more friction? What kind makes less friction?

How Do Wheels Help Objects Move?

Rollers

You will need

rollers   heavy book   toy truck   tape

1 Push the book. Then put rollers under it. Push again. Which is easier?

2 Push the truck. Tape the wheels, and push it again. Which is easier?

3 Draw a conclusion about wheels and rollers.

Science Skill

To draw a conclusion about something, use what you have observed to explain what happens.

What Wheels Can Do

A roller is any object that rolls. A **wheel** is a roller that turns on an axle. Rollers and wheels make things easier to push or pull.

Many Ways to Use Wheels

People use wheels in many ways. They use baskets on wheels to carry things when they shop. They use chairs on wheels to help them move around. Some children put wheels on boxes to make play cars.

People use wheels to help them push or pull loads. A dolly's wheels make it easy to push heavy boxes. Many suitcases have wheels so that people can pull them along.

■ **Why do people use things that have wheels?**

Think About It

1. What is a wheel?

2. What can wheels do?

An Architect Plans Buildings

I. M. Pei designs buildings. He knows about forces that push and pull. He designs buildings that won't fall down.

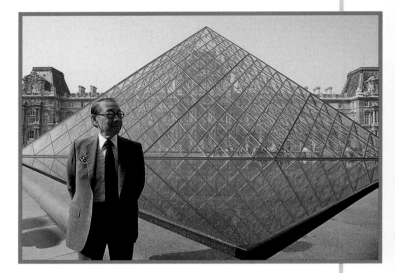

Think and Do 🖐

Use index cards to build a house. Then blow on your house of cards. Find different ways to make a house you can not blow down.

E26

Math Link

Push for Points

In some games, players use pushes to score points. Air hockey and bowling are two games like this.

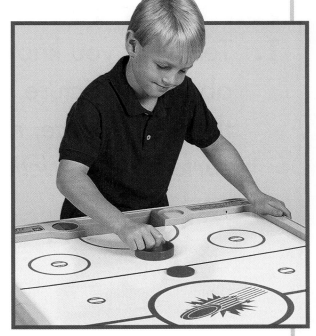

Think and Do

Make a game that uses pushes to score points. Use a box lid. Then use a pencil to flip a bottle cap ten times into the lid.

Add the number it lands on to your score each time.

Tell What You Know

1. Tell what you know about the picture. Use the words *force*, *motion*, *surface*, and *friction*.

Vocabulary

Tell which picture goes with each word.

2. push
3. pull
4. zigzag
5. wheel

a.

b.

c.

d.

Using Science Skills

6. Measure Pull a rock across rough and smooth surfaces with a rubber band. Measure how long the rubber band stretches each time. Make a chart. Record the numbers. Which makes more friction?

Friction on Surfaces	
Surface	How Long the Rubber Band Stretches
rough	
smooth	

7. Draw a Conclusion Rub your hands together. Feel the friction. Then put a few drops of oil on your hands. Rub again. Draw a conclusion.

CHAPTER 2

Magnets

Vocabulary

magnet

attract

strength

repel

poles

magnetic force

magnetize

Did You Know?
The Maglev train is run by **magnets**.

Did You Know?
These magnets can **repel** each other.

E31

What Are Magnets?

What a Magnet Can Do

You will need

bar magnet

objects

paper and pencil

What a Magnet Can Do		
Object	Pulls	Does Not Pull

1 Gather data about the magnet. Hold it near each object.

2 Make a chart like this one. Record what you observe.

3 Group the objects the magnet pulls and those it does not pull.

Science Skill

To gather data about what a magnet can do, observe and record what it does.

Magnets

A **magnet** is a piece of iron that can **attract**, or pull, things. The things it pulls must also be made of iron. Iron is a kind of metal.

■ **How are magnets used here?**

How People Use Magnets

People use magnets to hold things closed and to lift things. They also use them in televisions and electric motors.

A farmer may put a magnet in a cow's stomach. The magnet attracts bits of metal that the cow may eat. This keeps the metal from hurting the cow.

cow magnet

Where Magnets Can Be Found

Some magnets are found in nature. Lodestone is a kind of magnet found in the ground.

lodestone

■ How are the children using magnets in this fishing game?

How Magnets Are the Same and Different

Magnets are the same in one way. They attract objects made of iron. They do not attract objects made of other materials.

Magnets may be different in other ways. They may be round or square, big or small, straight or curved. They may be different colors.

Magnets may be different in **strength**, or how strongly they pull. One magnet may attract more paper clips than another.

■ **Look at the chart. Which magnet has the greater strength?**

Magnet Strength	
Magnet	Number of Clips
bar magnet	6
horseshoe magnet	3

Think About It

1. What is a magnet?

2. What are some ways people use magnets?

What Are the Poles of a Magnet?

A Magnet's Ends

You will need

bar magnet

paper clips

paper and pencil

1 Pick up paper clips with one end of the magnet. Record the number. Then do the other end.

2 Pick up paper clips with the middle of the magnet. Record the number.

3 Make a bar graph. Infer which parts of the magnet are strongest.

Science Skill

To infer which parts of the magnet are the strongest, compare the numbers in your bar graph.

The Poles of a Magnet

A magnet has two **poles**. These are the places where its pulling force is strongest. Where are the poles of this bar magnet? How can you tell?

What Poles Can Do

Every magnet has a north pole and a south pole. They are often called the *N* pole and the *S* pole.

Two poles that are different attract each other. An *N* pole and an *S* pole attract each other.

Two poles that are the same **repel**, or push away, each other. Two *N* poles repel each other.

■ **What do you think two *S* poles would do?**

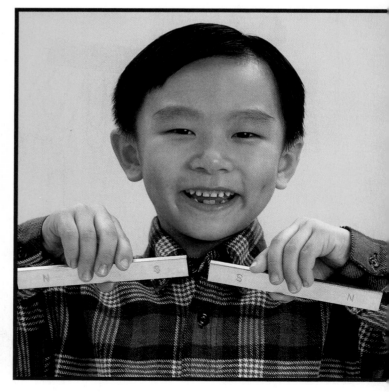

Bits of iron can show where a magnet's pull is strongest. The iron bits make a pattern around the magnet. More bits go to the poles, where the pull is strongest.

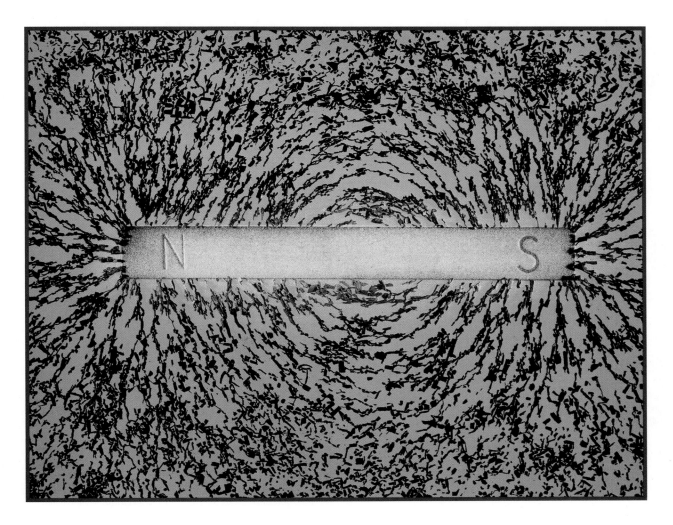

Think About It

1. What are poles?
2. What do poles do?

What Can a Magnet Pull Through?

Things Magnets Pull Through

You will need

bar magnet

paper clips

different materials

1 Can a magnet attract paper clips through things? Plan an investigation to find out. Write your plan.

2 Follow your plan to investigate your ideas. Record what you observe.

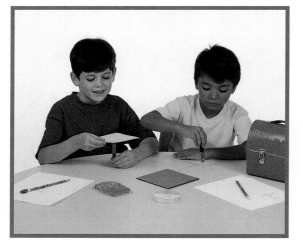

3 Use your data to communicate what you find out.

Science Skill

To investigate what things a magnet can pull through, first make a plan and then try your ideas.

The Force of a Magnet

A magnet's pull is called **magnetic force**. This force can pass through some things to attract iron objects.

■ **What material is magnetic force passing through to attract these puppets?**

Observing Magnetic Force

The magnetic force of a magnet can pass through paper. It can also pass through water and glass.

■ **What do you think might happen if the glass were thicker?**

Magnetic force is strong close to a magnet. It can pull a paper clip through the air. Farther away, it may not be strong enough to do this.

Think About It

1. What is magnetic force?
2. What are some materials magnetic force can pass through?

How Can You Make a Magnet?

Investigate

Making a Magnet

You will need

magnet

2 paper clips

1 Touch one clip to the other. Observe.

2 Use the magnet to pick up one clip. Touch that clip to the other one. Observe.

3 Take away the magnet. Draw a conclusion. How can you make a magnet?

Science Skill

To draw a conclusion, use what you have observed to form an idea.

Making a Magnet

A magnet can **magnetize**, or give magnetic force to, things it attracts. The magnet on this crane has magnetized some pieces of metal. Their new magnetic force attracts more pieces.

Ways to Make a Magnet

You can magnetize an iron nail. Stroke the nail on the magnet ten times the same way. Then the nail will be magnetized for a short time.

■ **How can you tell that this nail is now a magnet?**

Some magnets are made from iron heated with other materials. These magnets are made in a factory.

A magnet engineer finds new ways to make magnets. These magnets may be stronger or last longer than iron ones.

Think About It

1. What can you use to magnetize an object made of iron?
2. How can you make a magnet?

Math Link

Measure Magnetic Force

You can compare the strengths of different magnets. To do this, you will need to record how far their magnetic forces reach.

Think and Do

Lay a paper clip at one end of a paper strip. Hold one magnet at the other end. Slide the magnet slowly toward the clip. Make a mark to show where the magnet is when the clip moves.

Do the same thing with each magnet. Which magnet is the strongest?

Compass Readings

Long ago, travelers used compasses to find their way. Travelers still use them today. A compass has a magnetized needle that always points north.

Think and Do

Make your own compass. Float a plastic plate in water. Place a bar magnet in the center of the plate. Turn the plate. Which way is north?

Tell What You Know

1. Use the words *strength*, *poles*, and *magnetic force* to tell about each picture.

Vocabulary

Tell which picture goes with each word.

2. magnet

3. attract

4. repel

5. magnetize

a.

b.

c.

d.

Using Science Skills

6. **Infer** Look at the two patterns made by the bits of iron. Which magnet made each pattern? How do you know?

7. **Investigate** Some people use a metal detector to help them find things made of metal.

Play a metal detector game. Ask a partner to put three metal objects in a group of objects.

Predict which objects your magnet will attract. Investigate to find out.

Magnetic Kite

1. Cut out a tissue paper kite.

2. Attach thread and a paper clip.

3. Tape the thread's tail to a table.

4. Use the magnet to pick up your kite without touching it.

Magnetic Race-Car Game

1. Draw a road on cardboard.

2. Put two paper clips on the road.

3. Put two magnets under the cardboard. Move the magnets to race your clips.

Make a Water Wheel

1. Push toothpicks into the ends of a piece of clay. *Be careful. Toothpicks are sharp.*

2. Push strips cut from a carton into the clay to make a water wheel.

3. Hold the wheel by the toothpicks. Place the wheel under running water.

4. Tell how the water makes the wheel turn.

Marble Fun Slide

1. Tape together paper towel tubes to make a fun slide.

2. Use books to hold up the tubes.

3. Put a marble at the top, and listen to it race to the bottom. Talk about how it moves.

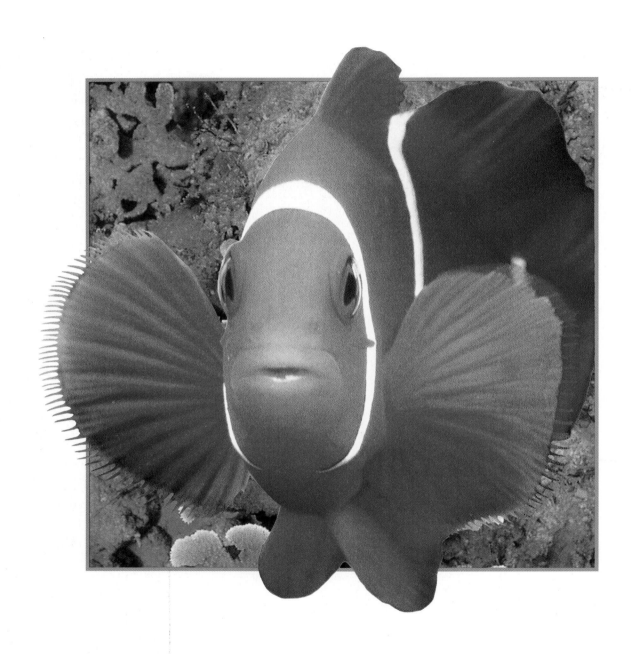

E56

References

Investigating

This plan will help you work like a scientist.

STEP 1 — Ask a question.

Which car will roll the farthest?

STEP 2 — Make a prediction.

I predict this car will win.

STEP 3 — Plan a fair test.

I'll start each car at the same spot.

STEP 4 — Do your test.

I'll measure how far each car rolls.

STEP 5 — Draw a conclusion.

My prediction was correct! This car rolled the farthest.

Investigate More

I wonder if the height of the ramp will make a difference.

Using Science Tools

Hand Lens

1. Hold the hand lens close to your face.
2. Move the object until you see it clearly.

Thermometer

1. Place the thermometer.
2. Wait two minutes.
3. Find the top of the liquid in the tube.
4. Read the number.

The temperature is 40 degrees.

Ruler

1. Put the beginning of the ruler at one end of the object.

2. Look at the number at the other end.

3. Read how long the object is.

This leaf is
21 centimeters long.

Measuring Cup

1. Pour the liquid into the cup.
2. Put the cup on a table.
3. Wait until the liquid is still.
4. Look at the level of the liquid.
5. Read how much liquid there is.

The cup has 150 milliliters of liquid in it.

Clock

1. Look at the hour hand.
2. Look at the minute hand.
3. Read the time.

It is 10:00.

Stopwatch

1. To start timing, press START.
2. To stop timing, press STOP.
3. Read how much time has passed.

Now 15 seconds have gone by.

Balance

1. Start with the pans even.
2. Put the object in one pan.
3. Add masses until the pans are even again.
4. Count up the number of masses.

Computer

1. A computer can help you draw or make charts.

2. Most computers help you find answers to questions.

3. Many computers help you communicate.

Measurements

1 cm

centimeter (cm) ruler

1 in.

inch (in.) ruler

Water freezes at 32°F.

Fahrenheit (F)
temperature

Water freezes at 0°C.

Celsius (C)
temperature

1 kilogram (kg)

1 pound (lb)

1 liter (L)

1 cup (c)

Health Handbook

Caring for Your Body

Staying Safe

Eyes and Ears

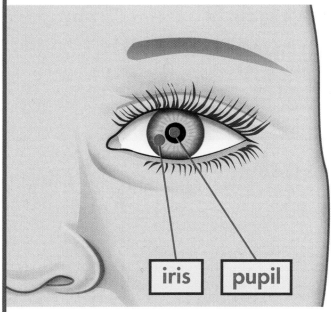

Outside of Eye

iris   pupil

Caring for Your Eyes and Ears

- Some bright light can hurt your eyes. Never look at the sun or at very bright lights.
- Never put an object in your ear.

Eyes

When you look at your eyes, you can see a white part, a colored part, and a dark center. The colored part is the iris. The dark center is the pupil.

Inside of Eye

iris

pupil

Ear

Your ears let you hear. Most of each ear is inside your head.

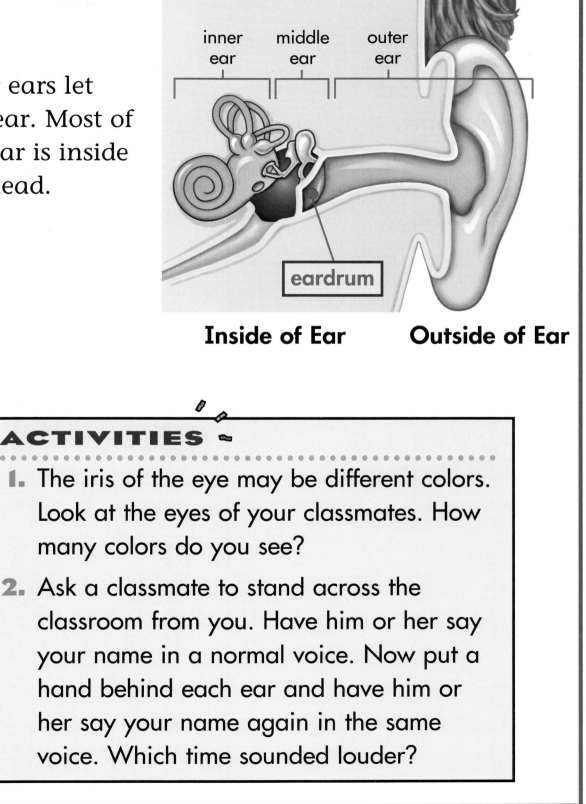

inner ear   middle ear   outer ear

eardrum

Inside of Ear   **Outside of Ear**

ACTIVITIES

1. The iris of the eye may be different colors. Look at the eyes of your classmates. How many colors do you see?

2. Ask a classmate to stand across the classroom from you. Have him or her say your name in a normal voice. Now put a hand behind each ear and have him or her say your name again in the same voice. Which time sounded louder?

The Skeletal System

Inside your body are hard, strong bones. They make up your skeleton. Your skeleton holds you up.

Caring for Your Skeletal System

Protect your head. Wear a helmet when you ride your bike.

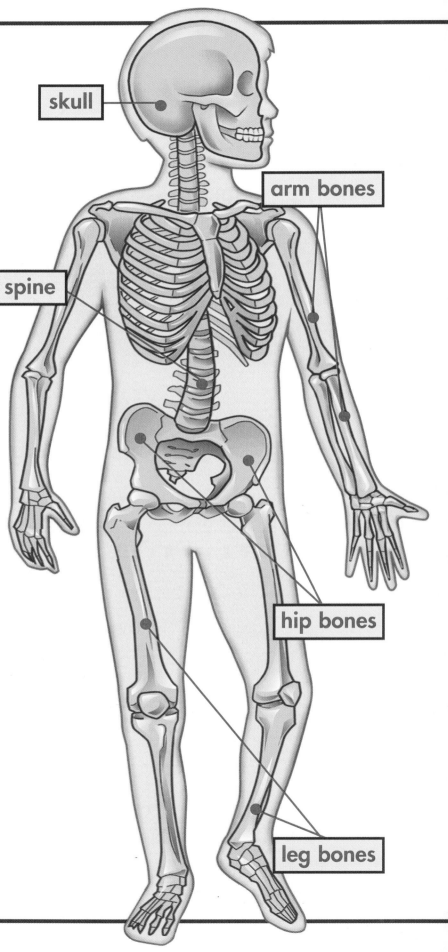

skull

arm bones

spine

hip bones

leg bones

skull

spine

Skull

The bones in your head are called your skull. Your skull protects your brain.

Spine

Your spine, or backbone, is made up of many small bones. Your spine helps you stand up straight.

ACTIVITIES

1. Look at a bike helmet. How is it like your skull?

2. Your foot is about the same length as your arm between your hand and your elbow. Put your foot on your arm and check it out!

The Digestive System

Your digestive system helps your body get energy from the food you eat.

Caring for Your Digestive System

- Brush and floss your teeth every day.

- Don't eat right before you exercise. Your body needs energy to digest food.

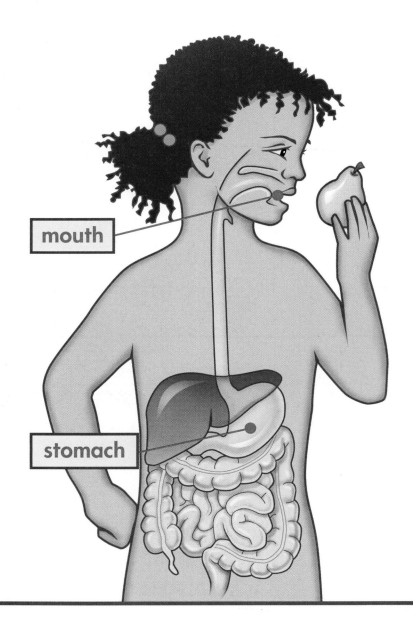

mouth

stomach

Teeth

Some of your teeth tear food and some grind it into small parts.

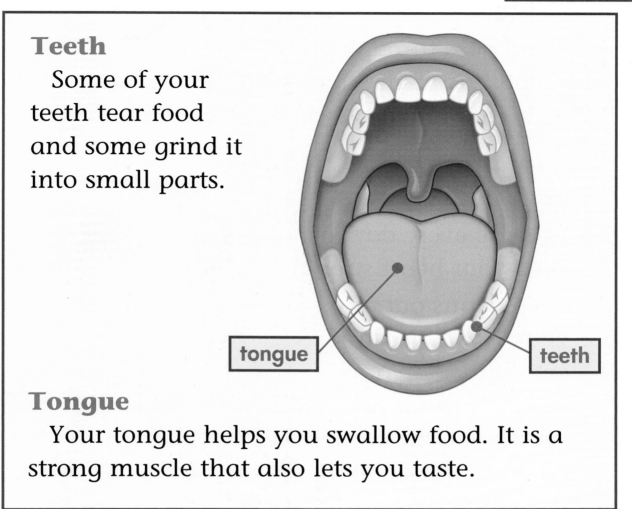

tongue

teeth

Tongue

Your tongue helps you swallow food. It is a strong muscle that also lets you taste.

ACTIVITIES

1. Bite into an apple and chew the bite. Which teeth did you use for these jobs?

2. Lick a salty pretzel and a lollipop. Which one can you taste better with just the tip of your tongue?

The Circulatory System

Blood goes through your body in your circulatory system. Your heart pumps the blood. Your blood vessels carry the blood.

Caring for Your Circulatory System

- Exercise every day to keep your heart strong.
- Keep germs out of your blood. Wash cuts with soap and water. Never touch someone else's blood.

blood vessels

heart

Heart

Your heartbeat is the sound of your heart pumping. Your heart is about the same size as a fist.

fist

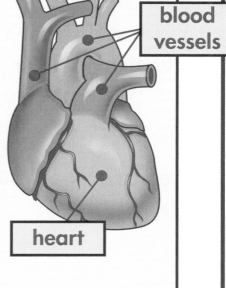

blood vessels

heart

Blood Vessels

Blood vessels are tubes that carry blood through your body.

ACTIVITIES

1. Ask an adult to blow up a hot-dog shaped balloon so that it is not quite full. Squeeze one end. What happens?

2. Put your ear to the middle of a classmate's chest and listen to the heartbeat. Then listen again through a paper cup with the bottom torn out. Which way of listening works better?

The Respiratory System

When you breathe, you are using your respiratory system. Your mouth, your nose, and your lungs are parts of your respiratory system.

Caring for Your Respiratory System

- Never put anything in your nose.

- Exercise makes you breathe harder and is good for your lungs.

nose

mouth

lungs

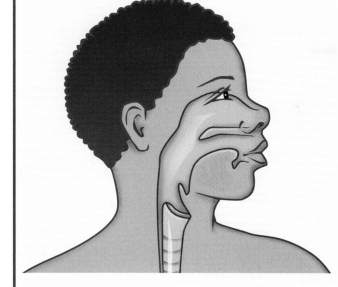

Mouth and Nose

Air goes in and out of your body through your mouth and nose.

Lungs

You have two lungs in your chest. When you breathe in, your lungs fill with air. When you breathe out, air leaves your lungs.

ACTIVITIES

1. Watch your chest and stomach muscles as you take a breath and let it out. Describe what happens.

2. Count how many breaths you take in one minute.

The Muscular System

The muscles in your body help you move.

Caring for Your Muscular System

Warm up your muscles before you play or exercise.

ACTIVITY

Hold your arm straight out from your body and lift it over your head. Then try it again with a book in your hand. How do the muscles in your arm feel?

face muscles

neck muscles

arm muscles

stomach muscles

leg muscles

The Nervous System

brain

nerves

Your nervous system keeps your body working and tells you about things around you. Your brain is part of your nervous system.

Caring for Your Nervous System

Get plenty of sleep. Sleeping lets your brain rest.

ACTIVITY

Clap your hands in front of a classmate's face. What happens to his or her eyes?

Staying Safe

Fire Safety

You can stay safe from fires. Follow these safety rules.

- Never play with matches or lighters.
- Be careful around stoves, heaters, fireplaces, and grills.
- Don't use microwaves, irons, or toasters without an adult's help.
- Practice your family's fire safety plan.
- If there is a fire in your home, get out quickly. Drop to the floor and crawl if the room is filled with smoke. If a closed door feels hot, don't open it. Use another exit. Call 911 from outside your home.
- If your clothes catch on fire, use Stop, Drop, and Roll right away to put out the flames.

❶ Stop Don't run or wave your arms.

❷ Drop Lie down quickly. Cover your eyes with your hands.

❸ Roll Roll back and forth to put out the fire.

Stranger Danger

You can stay safe around strangers. Follow these rules.

- Never talk to strangers.
- Never go with a stranger, on foot or in a car.
- If you are home alone, do not open the door. Do not let telephone callers know you are alone.
- Never give your name, address, or phone number to anyone you don't know. (You may give this information to a 911 operator in an emergency.)
- If you are lost or need help, talk to a police officer, a guard, or a store clerk.
- If a stranger bothers you, use the Stranger Danger rules to stay safe.

❶ **Say no!** Yell if you need to. You do not have to be polite to strangers.

❷ **Get away.** Walk fast or run in the opposite direction. Go toward people who can help you.

❸ **Tell someone.** Tell a trusted adult, such as a family member, a teacher, or a police officer. Do not keep secrets about strangers.

Staying Safe
A Safe Bike

To ride your bike safely, you need to start with a safe bike. A safe bike is the right size for you. When you sit on your bike with the pedal in the lowest position, you should be able to rest your heel on the pedal.

After checking the size of your bike, check to see that it has the right safety equipment. Your bike should have everything shown below.

horn

white reflector

red reflector

clear reflector

clear reflector

reflectors

Your Bike Helmet

◄ Always wear a bike helmet. Wear your helmet flat on your head. Be sure it is strapped tightly. If your helmet gets bumped in a fall, replace it right away, even if it doesn't look damaged.

Safety on the Road

- Check your bike for safety every time you ride it.
- Ride in single file. Ride in the same direction as traffic.
- Stop, look, listen, and think when you enter a street or cross a driveway.
- Walk your bike across an intersection.
- Obey all traffic signs and signals.
- Don't ride at night without an adult. Wear light-colored clothing and use lights and reflectors for night riding.

GLOSSARY

A

algae

An ocean plant. (A118)

amphibian

An animal with smooth, wet skin. (A52)

attract

To pull something. (E33)

C

change

To make different. (C21)

condense

To change from water vapor into tiny drops of water. (B18)

D

desert

A dry place. (A109)

E

enrich

To make better. (A90)

float

To stay on top of a liquid. (C13)

evaporate

To change from water into water vapor. (B18)

flower

The part of a plant that makes seeds. (A27)

F

fall

The season that follows summer. (B35)

force

A push or a pull. (E5)

forest

A place where many trees grow. (A105)

gills

Body part that helps a fish take air from water. (A47)

friction

A force that makes it harder to move things. (E20)

H

hatch

To break out of an egg. (A60)

G

gas

Matter that does not have a shape of its own, such as air. (C17)

heat

What is given off by the sun and warms Earth's land, air, and water. (C35)

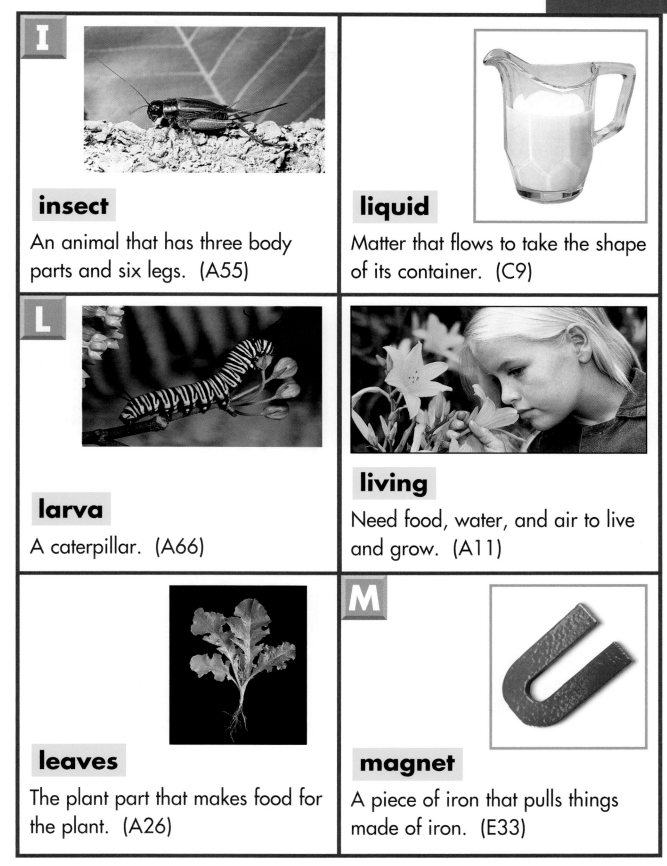

I

insect
An animal that has three body parts and six legs. (A55)

liquid
Matter that flows to take the shape of its container. (C9)

L

larva
A caterpillar. (A66)

living
Need food, water, and air to live and grow. (A11)

leaves
The plant part that makes food for the plant. (A26)

M

magnet
A piece of iron that pulls things made of iron. (E33)

magnetic force

The pulling force of a magnet. (E43)

matter

Everything around you. (C5)

magnetize

To give magnetic force to something a magnet attracts. (E47)

mechanic

A person who can fix a broken car part or put in a new one. (C27)

mammal

An animal that has hair or fur and feeds its young milk. (A50)

melt

To change from a solid to a liquid. (C40)

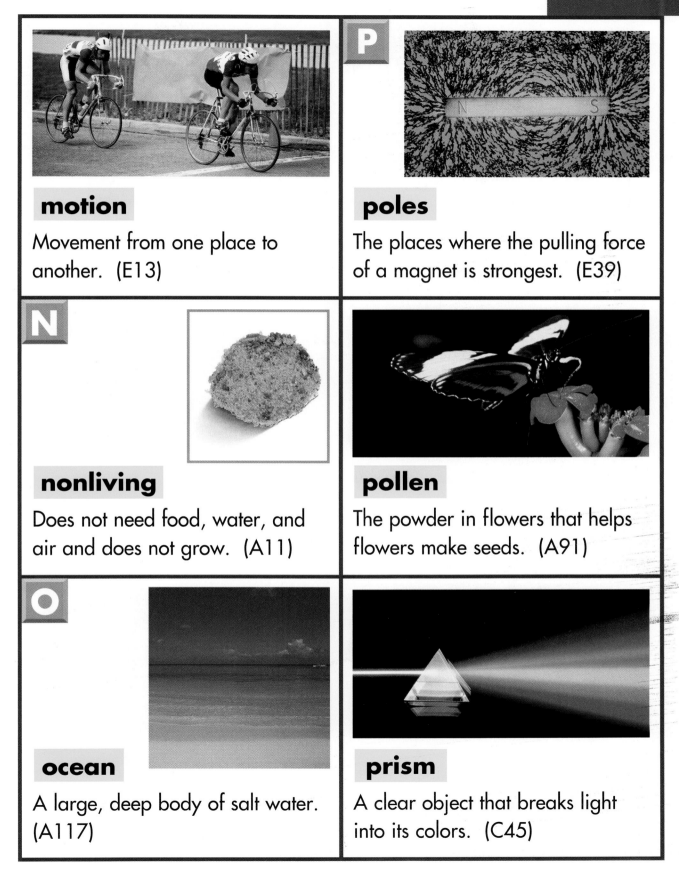

motion

Movement from one place to another. (E13)

P

poles

The places where the pulling force of a magnet is strongest. (E39)

N

nonliving

Does not need food, water, and air and does not grow. (A11)

pollen

The powder in flowers that helps flowers make seeds. (A91)

O

ocean

A large, deep body of salt water. (A117)

prism

A clear object that breaks light into its colors. (C45)

product

Something that people make from other things. (A94)

push

To press something away. (E5)

pull

To tug something closer. (E5)

R

rain forest

A forest that is wet all year. (A113)

pupa

A hard covering over a caterpillar. (A67)

reflect

To bounce back light. (C48)

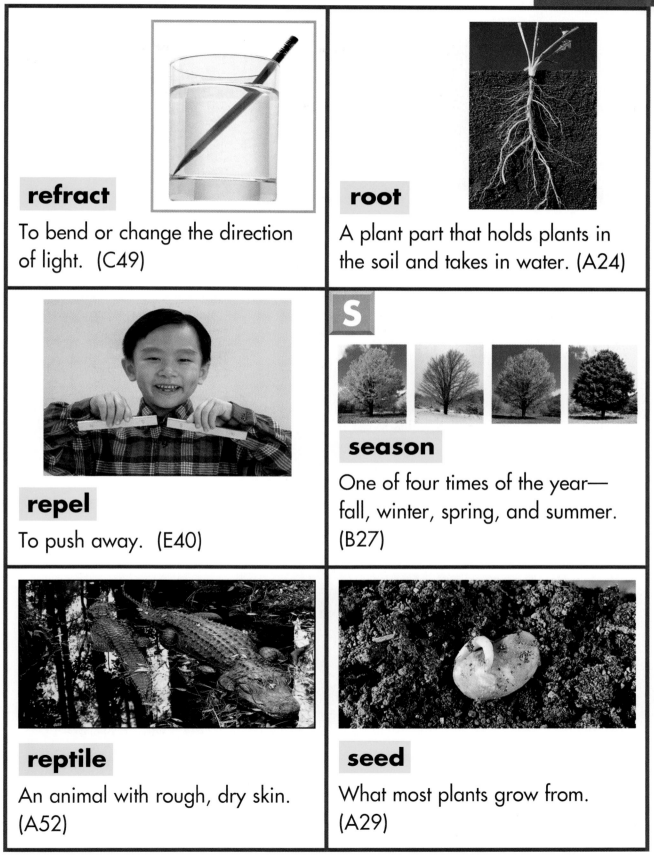

refract

To bend or change the direction of light. (C49)

root

A plant part that holds plants in the soil and takes in water. (A24)

repel

To push away. (E40)

S

season

One of four times of the year—fall, winter, spring, and summer. (B27)

reptile

An animal with rough, dry skin. (A52)

seed

What most plants grow from. (A29)

R35

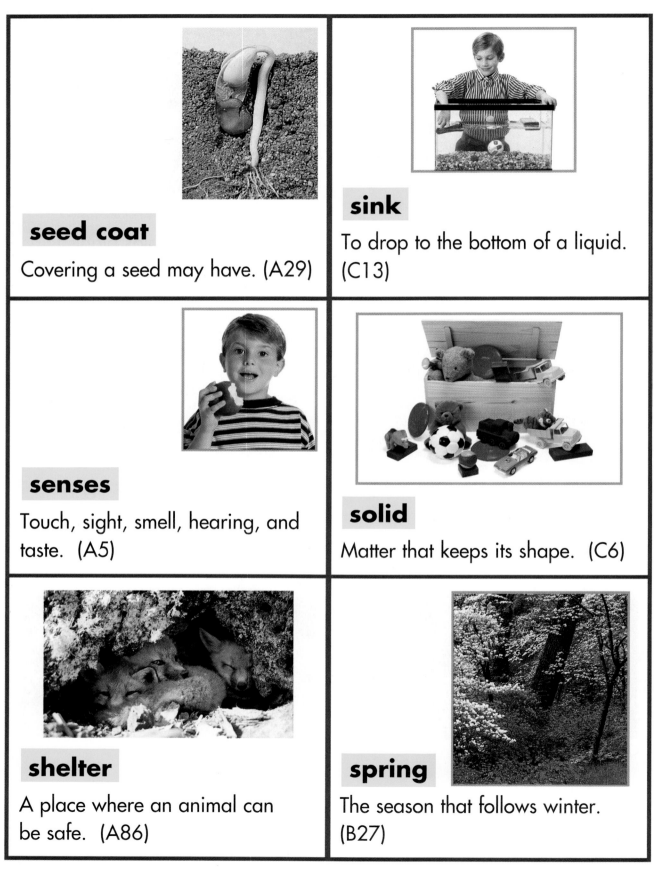

seed coat
Covering a seed may have. (A29)

sink
To drop to the bottom of a liquid. (C13)

senses
Touch, sight, smell, hearing, and taste. (A5)

solid
Matter that keeps its shape. (C6)

shelter
A place where an animal can be safe. (A86)

spring
The season that follows winter. (B27)

stem

Plant part that helps hold up the plant and moves water to the leaves. (A25)

sunlight

Light from the sun. (A34)

strength

How strong something is, such as a magnet's pull. (E37)

surface

The top or outside of something. (E19)

summer

The season that follows spring. (B31)

T

tadpole

A young frog that hatches from an egg. (A72)

temperature

The measure of how hot or cold something is. (B9)

water vapor

Water that you can not see in the air. (B18)

thermometer

A tool that measures temperature. (B9)

weather

What the air outside is like. (B5)

W

water cycle

The movement of water from the Earth to the sky and back again. (B18)

wheel

A roller that turns on an axle. (E23)

wind

Moving air. (B13)

winter

The season that follows fall. (B39)

Z

zigzag

Make sharp turns back and forth. (E10)

A

Adams, Ansel, B42

Air
animals need, A43,
A47
a gas, C16, C18, C19
and light movement,
C47
plants need, A33,
A34, A35
temperature, B8,
B9–B11, B20
water in, B18–B19
and weather, B5, B6
wind, B13–B15

Amphibians, A49,
A52
frogs, A70, A71–A73
salamander, A52

Animals
caring for young,
A62–A63
desert, A111
in fall, B37
forest, A107
growth, A58, A59,
A60–A61, A64–A67,
A70–A73
homes, A42, A43,
A46
kinds of, A48, A49
needs, A42,
A43–A47
nests, A83, A87,
A107
ocean, A116, A119
pets and helpers, A97

and plants, A82,
A83–A87, A88,
A89–A91
rain forest, A113–A115
in spring, B29
in summer, B33
used by people, A92,
A93, A96–A97
in winter, B41
See also
Amphibians; Birds;
Fish; Insects;
Mammals; Reptiles

Architect, E26

Artist
Pablo Picasso, C28
Vincent van Gogh,
A36

Attract, E33, E36, E40

B

Balloon, hot air, C41,
C50

Bike safety, R26–R27

Birds, A49, A51
bluebird, A51
cactus wren, A110
chickens, A60–A61
emperor penguin, A63
flamingo, A51
macaw, A51, A114
mallard duck, A43
nest, A87
oriole, A87
peregrine falcon, A46
robin, A62
toucan, A85
wood thrush, A107

**Blood vessels,
in circulatory
system,** R18, R19

Body, senses, A4–A9

Body systems
circulatory, R18–R19
digestive, R16–R17
muscular, R22
nervous, R23
respiratory, R20–R21
senses organs,
R12–R13
skeletal, R14–R15

Brain
in nervous system,
R23
protected, R15

Breathing
respiratory system,
R20–R21

**Buildings, and
force,** E26

Butterfly, A57
growth, A64,
A65–A67
helping plants, A91
wings, A68–A69,
A75

C

D

E

F

Magnet engineer,
E49

Magnetic force,
E43–E45
giving metal, E47,
E48–E49
measuring, E50

Magnetize, E47,
E48–E49

Magnets, E32, E33,
E42
in compass, E51
kinds of, E36
lodestone, E35
making, E46, E47,
E48–E49
measuring strength,
E50
poles, E38–E41
strength, E37
uses, E34

Mammals, A49, A50
African leopard, A86
armadillo, A111
bat, A46
bear, A62
bottle-nosed dolphin,
A118
camel, A45
chimpanzee, A62
cow, A47, A84
deer mouse, A87
elephant, A45
horse, A44
kangaroo rat, A111
mountain lion, A44

pig, A50
rabbit, A60–A61,
A83, A84
raccoon, A85
red fox, A107
sheep, A96
sloth, A114
squirrel, A50
whitetail deer, A50

Marine biologist,
A121

Matter, C5
changed by heat,
C39–C41
gases, C17–C19
liquids, C9–C11
solids, C6–C7

Mechanic, C27

Melt, C39, C40

Meteorologist, B7

Mix
objects, C23
to make art, C28

Motion, E13
changing, E14–E15

Mouse, nest, A87

Movement, E9–E11
as motion, E13
by push or pull, E5,
E6–E7

Muscular system, R22

Needs
animal, A42,
A43–A47
people, A92,
A93–A96
plant, A32–A35

Nervous system, R23

Nests, A83, A87,
A107

Nonliving things,
A10, A11, A13,
A14–A15

**North pole
(of magnet),** E40

N pole, E40

Objects
changing, C21–C23
floating or sinking,
C13–C15
parts of, C25–C26

Ocean, A117,
animals, A116,
A118–A119
plants, A118
scientist, A121

Parks, A46

Parts
    of objects, C25–C26

Path, E10

Patterns
    in leaves, A120
    weather, B21

People
    using plants and
    animals, A92,
    A93–A97

Pets, A97

Photographer, B42

Picasso, Pablo, C28

Pig, A50

Plants
    algae, A118
    and animals, A82,
    A83–A87, A88,
    A89–A91
    in art, A36
    beavertail cactus,
    A110
    berry bush, A106
    bromeliad, A115
    cotton, A94
    desert, A108, A110
    in fall, B34, B36
    as food, A95, A98
    forest, A106
    growth, A29–A31
    measuring, A37
    mountain laurel, A106
    needs, A32–A35

ocean, A118
orchid, A115
parts, A22, A23–A27
rain forest, A112,
    A115
seeds, A29, A30–A31
in spring, B28
in summer, B32
uses, A92, A93,
    A94–A95, A99
in winter, B40
yucca, A110

Poles, magnet,
    E38–E41

Pollen, A91

Prism, C45

Product, A94–A96

Pull, E5
    changing direction,
    E16–E17
    changing motion,
    E14–E15
    with wheel, E23

Pull, magnetic, E33,
    E37, E39, E41,
    E43–E45

Pupa, A67

Pupil, R12

Puppets, shadow,
    C51

Push, E5, E6, E7
    changing direction
    E16–E17
    changing motion,
    E14–E15
    in games, E27
    with wheel, E23

Rabbits
    food for, A83, A84
    growth, A60–A61

Rain, B17
    graphing, B43
    in spring, B27
    in the water cycle, B19

Rain forest, A113
    animals, A114
    plants, A112, A115

Reflect, C48

Refract, C49

Repel, E40

Reptiles, A49, A52
    alligator, A52, A87
    box turtle, A107
    giant tortoise, A52
    rattlesnake, A111
    sea turtle, A119

Respiratory system,
    R20–R21

Rollers, E22, E23

Roots, A23, A24

**Rubbing, making
    heat,** C37

Photography Credits: Page placement key: (t) top, (c) center, (b) bottom, (l) left, (r) right, (bg) background, (i) inset

Cover: P. DeWilde/Liaison International; (bg) Norbert Wu.

Table of Contents: Pg. i P. DeWilde/Liaison International; i (bg) Norbert Wu; ii P. De Wilde/Liaison International; ii (bg) Norbert Wu.

Unit A: Pg. A1 Robert Canis/Masterfile; A1 (bg) Andre Gallant/The Image Bank; A2-A3 Ron Kimball Photography; A3 (i) Ray Mathis/The Stock Market; A5 Picture It; A6 David Waldorf/FPG International; A8-A9 (t) DiMaggio/Kalish/LThe Stock Market; A8 (b), A9 (b) Laura Dwight Photography; A11 Gene Peach/Index Stock; A12 (l) John Gerlach/Animals Animals/Earth Scenes; A12 (r) Mitsuaki Iwago/Minden Pictures; A13 (l) Barry L. Runk/Grant Heilman Photography, Inc.; A13 (r) Michael Groen Photography; A14 (l) Victoria Hurst/Tom Stack & Associates; A14 (r) Laura Dwight/Peter Arnold, Inc.; A15 (l) Werner H. Muller/Peter Arnold, Inc.; A15 (r) Jeff Foott/Bruce Coleman, Inc.; A17 Stephen Ogilvy/Picture It; A18 (tl) Tony Freeman/PhotoEdit; A18 (tlc) Michael Groen Photography; A18 (tc) Sonya Jacobs/The Stock Market; A18 (trc) George Mattei/LEnvision; A18 (tr) John Fowler/Valan Photos; A18 (brc) A. Ramage/Animals/Animals/Earth Scenes; A19 Michael Groen Photography; A20-A21 Frans Lanting/Minden Pictures; A21 (i) Richard Shiell/Animals Animals/Earth Scenes; A25 (r) Bill Bachman/Photo Researchers; A26 (tl), A26 (br) Runk/Schoenberger/Grant Heilman Photography, Inc.; A26 tc) Greg Vaughn/Tom Stack & Associates; A26 (tr) Don Mason/The Stock Market; A26 (bl) Colin Milkins/Animals Animals/Earth Scenes; A27 Rich Miller/AG Stock USA; A29 (tr) Joseph Nettis/Stock, Boston; A29 (cr) D. Cavagnaro/Visuals Unlimited; A29 (bl) Paul Barton/The Stock Market; A29 (br) Michael Groen Photography; A30 (tl) Stephen J. Krasemann/DRK Photo; A30 (bl) Barry L. Runk/Grant Heilman Photography, Inc.; A30 (br) Inga Spence/Tom Stack; A30 (cr) Ed Young/AG Stock USA; A30 (tl) Gerard Lacz/Peter Arnold, Inc.; A30 (tr) Ed Young/AG Stock USA; A30-A31 Tom Bean/DRK Photo; A31 (bl) G.I. Bernard/Animals Animals/Earth Scenes; A31 (br) Runk/Schoenberger/Grant Heilman Photography, Inc.; A31 (cl) Barry L. Runk/Grant Heilman Photography, Inc.; A31 (tl) Runk/Schoenberger/Grant Heilman Photography, Inc.; A31 (tr) D. Trask/The Stock Market; A33 Glenn Oakley/AG Stock USA; A35 (l) Larry Ulrich/Tony Stone Images; A35 (r) Bill Brooks/Masterfile; A36 (i) National Gallery London/Superstock; A38 (a) Superstock; A38 (b) Jerry Howard/Positive Images; A38 (c) Tim McKenna/The Stock Market; A38 (d) Lynwood M. Chase/Photo Researchers; A38 (e) T. A. Wiewandt/DRK Photo; A38 (f) D. Cavagnaro/Visuals Unlimited; A38 (top-all), A38 (g), A39 (b) Runk/Schoenberger/Grant Heilman Photography, Inc.; A39 (t) Fred Bruemmer/DRK Photo; A40-A41 Kim Taylor/Bruce Coleman, Inc.; A41 (tl) J. C. Carton/Bruce Coleman, Inc.; A41 (tr) Hans Reinhard/Bruce Coleman, Inc.; A41 (bl) Michael Fogden/DRK Photo; A43 S. Nielsen/DRK Photo; A44 (tl) Dick Canby/DRK Photo; A44 (tr) Steve Bly/Tony Stone Images; A44 (bl) Tom Tietz/Tony Stone Images; A44 (tr) Hans Reinhard/Bruce Coleman, Inc.; A45 (t) Belinda Wright/DRK Photo; A45 (b) Frans Lanting/Minden Pictures; A46 (t) Merlin Tuttle/Photo Researchers; A46 (c) Ralph Ginzburg/Peter Arnold, Inc.; A46 (b) Lawrence Migdale; A47 (l) Ken Howard/The Wildlife Collection; A47 (r) G. I. Bernard/Animals Animals/Earth Scenes; A49 (bc) Jane Burton/Bruce Coleman, Inc.; A49 (br) Joe McDonald/Tom Stack & Associates; A49 (bl) Patricia Doyle/Tony Stone Images; A49 (tc) Lemoine Jacana/Photo Researchers; A49 (r) Marian Bacon/Animals Animals/Earth Scenes; A50 (t) Stephen J. Krasemann/DRK Photo; A50 (bl) Ed Reschke/Peter Arnold, Inc.; A50 (br) M. Rutz/Natural Selection; A51 (tl) Anthony Mercieca/Photo Researchers; A51 (tr) Frans Lanting/Minden Pictures; A51 (b) M. H. Sharp/Photo Researchers; A52 (t) David Muench/Tony Stone Images; A52 (c) Tui de Roy/Minden Pictures; A52 (b) Suzanne J. Collins/Photo Researchers; A53 (t) Charles V. Angelo/Photo Researchers; A53 (b) Brian Parker/Tom Stack & Associates; A55 John Mitchell/Photo Researchers; A56-A57 (b) Richard L. Carlton/Photo Researchers; A56 (t) A. Ramage/Animals Animals/Earth Scenes; A57 (t) Zefa/Brockhaus/The Stock Market; A57 (c) Robert & Linda Mitchell; A59 (t) Jane Burton/Bruce Coleman, Inc.; A59 (b) , A60 (bl), A60 (br), Jane Burton/DK Photos; A60 (tl), A60 (tr), A61 (tl) Jane Burton/Bruce Coleman, Inc.; A61 (tr), A61 (bl), A61 (br) Jane Burton/DK Photos; A62 (t) Bob Bennett/The Wildlife Collection; A62 (c) Robert Winslow/Natural Selection; A62 (b) John Giustina/The Wildlife Collection; A63 Stefan Lundgren/The Wildlife Collection; A65

Mesza/Bruce Coleman, Inc.; A66 (t) Ed Reschke/Peter Arnold, Inc.; A66 (b) Michael Fogden/DRK Photo; A67 (tl) Jeff Foott/DRK Photo; A67 (tr) D. Cavagnaro/DRK Photo; A67 (b) Harry Rogers/Photo Researchers; A68-A69 (c) Gary Vestal/Tony Stone Images; A68 (t) Sturgis McKeever/Photo Researchers; A68 (b) John Fowler/Valan Photos; A69 (t) Nancy Rotenberg/Animals Animals/Earth Scenes; A71 S. Dalton/Animals Animals/Earth Scenes; A72-A73 Michael Groen Photography; A72 (l) Brent P. Kent/Animals Animals/Earth Scenes; A72 (r) John M. Burnley/Photo Researchers; A72 (c), A73 (l) Runk/Schoenberger/Grant Heilman Photography, Inc.; A73 (r) Joe McDonald/Animals Animals/Earth Scenes; A74 Stephen Ogilvy/Picture It; A75 (t) Kjell Sandved/Butterfly Alphabet; A75 (b) Michael Groen Photography; A76 (top row left to right) (1) Patricia Doyle/Tony Stone Images; A76 (3) Breck P. Kent; A76 (4) David M. Dennis/Tom Stack & Assocites; A76 (5) Doug Wechsler/Animals Animals/Earth Scenes; A76 (6) J. H. Robinson/Animals Animals/Earth Scenes; A76 (bottom) (a). Jeff Foott/DRK Photo; (b). A. Ramage/Animals Animals/Earth Scenes; (c). Joe McDonald/Animals Animals/Earth Scenes; (d). Runk/Schoenberger/Grant Heilman Photography, Inc.; (e). Dick Canby/DRK Photos; (f). David Muench/Tony Stone Images; (g) Michael Fogden/DRK Photo; (h) Brian Parker/Tom Stack & Associates; (i) Jane Burton/DRK Photo; A77 Gary Vestal/Tony Stone Images; A80-A81 Gregory Ochocki/Photo Researchers; A81 (li) E. F. Anderson/Visuals Unlimited; A81 (ri) Roy Morsch/The Stock Market; Lynn M. Stone/Bruce Coleman, Inc.; A84 (l) Chris Jones/The Stock Market; A84 (r) Zefa-Brockhaus/The Stock Market; A85 (l) John Chellman/Animals Animals/Earth Scenes; A85 (r) Beth Davidow/Visuals Unlimited; A86 (t) Tom Brakefield/DRK Photo; A86 (b) Raymond A. Mendez/Animals Animals/Earth Scenes; A87 (t) Scott Nielsen/Bruce Coleman, Inc.; A87 (bl) Wendell Metzen/Bruce Coleman, Inc.; A87 (br) Jeff Foott/Bruce Coleman, Inc.; A90 (t) Patti Murray/Animals Animals/Earth Scenes; A90 (b) Breck P. Kent/Animals Animals/Earth Scenes; A91 Darlyne A. Murawski/Peter Arnold, Inc.; A93 Richard Hutchings/Picture It; A94 (t) Jon Feingersh/The Stock Market; A94 (c) Aaron Haupt/Photo Researchers; A94 (b) Pete Saloutos/The Stock Market; A95 (t) Stephen Ogilvy/Picture It; A95 (b) Hank Morgan/Rainbow; A96 (bl) Larry Lefever/Grant Heilman Photography, Inc.; A96 (br) Michael Groen Photography; A98 (b) Stephen Ogilvy/Picture It; A99 (t) Eric Horan; A99 (b) Michael Groen Photography; A100 (tl) Tom Bean/DRK Photo; A100 (tc) Hans Reinhard/Bruce Coleman, Inc.; A100 (tr) Tom Bean/Bruce Coleman, Inc.; A100 (cl) Darlyne A. Murawski; A100 (cr) Raymond A. Mendez/Animals Animals/Earth Scenes; A100 (bl) Breck P. Kent/Animals Animals/Earth Scenes; A100 (br) Michael Groen Photography; A102-A103 Jeremy Woodhouse/DRK Photo; A103 (i) Robert P. Carr/Bruce Coleman, Inc.; A105 Stephen J. Krasemann/DRK Photo; A106 (l) Pat OíHara/Tony Stone Images; A106 (r) James H. Robinson/Animals Animals/Earth Scenes; A107 (tl) Art Wolfe/Tony Stone Images; A107 (tr) Robert Lubeck/Animals Animals/Earth Scenes; A107 (b) R. A. Simpson/Visuals Unlimited; A109 Daniel J. Cox/Natural Exposures; A110 (t) Nora & Rick Bowers/The Wildlife Collection; A110 (bl) M. P. Kahl/DRK Photo; A110 (br) Jeff Foott/DRK Photo; A111 (t) Leonard Lee Rue III/Bruce Coleman, Inc.; A111 (c) Runk/Schoenberger/Grant Heilman Photography, Inc.; A111 (b) Joe McDonald/Animals Animals/Earth Scenes; A113 Michael Sewell/Peter Arnold, Inc.; A114 (l) Michael Fogden/DRK Photo; A114 (r) Ed Wheeler/The Stock Market; A115 (t) Softlight Photography/Animals Animals/Earth Scenes; A115 (b) David Matherly/Visuals Unlimited; A117 David Hall/Photo Researchers; A118-A119 Doug Perrine/DRK Photo; A118 (l) Soames Sommerhays/Photo Researchers; A119 (tr) Fred Winner/Jacana/Photo Researchers; A119 (br) Dave B. Fleetham/Visuals Unlimited; A120 (tl) Sullivan & Rogers/Bruce Coleman, Inc.; A120 (tc) Edgar T. Jones/Bruce Coleman, Inc.; A120 (tr) Patti Murray/Animals Animals/Earth Scenes; A121 (t) Tom & Therisa Stack/Tom Stack & Associates; A122 (tl) Stephen J. Krasemann/DRK Photo; A122 (tlc) Doug Perrine/DRK Photo; A122 (trc) Nora & Rick Bowers/The Wildlife Collection; A122 (tr) Ed Wheeler/The Stock Market; A122 (cl) Stephen J. Krasemann/DRK Photo; A122 (cc) John Kaprielian/Photo Researchers; A122 (cr) Randy Morse/Tom Stack & Associates; A122 (bl) Michael Seward/Peter Arnold, Inc.; A122 (br) Daniel J. Cox/Natural Exposures.

Unit B: Pg. B1 (t) Kevin Galvin/The Stock Market; B1 (b) Rod Planck/Photo Researchers; B1 (bg) Jeff Smith/Image Bank; B2-B3 Keith Kent/Science Source/Photo Researchers; B3 (i) Carl Wolinsky/Stock, Boston; B5 Stephen Ogilvy/Picture It; B5 (bg) Robert brenner/PhotoEdit; B6 (tl) J & M Studios/Gamma-Liaison International; B6 (tr) Timothy